Penguin Crossword Puz:

The Twelfth Penguin Book of
*The Times* Crosswords

# The Twelfth Penguin Book of
## *The Times* Crosswords

Penguin Books

PENGUIN BOOKS

Published by the Penguin Group
Penguin Books Ltd, 27 Wrights Lane, London W8 5TZ, England
Penguin Putnam Inc., 375 Hudson Street, New York, New York 10014, USA
Penguin Books Australia Ltd, Ringwood, Victoria, Australia
Penguin Books Canada Ltd, 10 Alcorn Avenue, Toronto, Ontario, Canada M4V 3B2
Penguin Books (NZ) Ltd, Private Bag 102902, NSMC, Auckland, New Zealand

Penguin Books Ltd, Registered Offices: Harmondsworth, Middlesex, England

First published in book form by Penguin Books 1990
10 9 8

Printed in England by Clays Ltd, St Ives plc
Filmset in Times

# Foreword

Experienced solvers of cryptic crosswords do not, in theory at least, need to check their answers, since each clue normally provides two separate routes to the answer, one of them a definition, thus enabling the solver to check for himself.

Nevertheless, on the evidence of *The Times* Collins Dictionaries championships, even the best solvers are sometimes stuck for an explanation: they usually get the right answers by inspired guesswork but cannot always see why.

It would be impracticable in a daily paper to add footnotes to the solution of yesterday's puzzle covering every possible query, though to avoid being overwhelmed with letters and telephone calls we did some months ago publish an explanatory footnote to the clue 'Telegraphed reply reported from Austerlitz, for example (3-6)'. The homophone 'tapped answer' was probably enough to give the average solver the answer TAP-DANCER, but why Austerlitz? This, as the note explained, was Fred Astaire's real name.

The puzzles in this book were published in *The Times* between January and June 1988, and the notes printed with the solutions at the back are intended primarily to elucidate references that may similarly be outside the reader's ken. More rarely, they explain the construction of a clue, and I apologise in advance if to some these seem to be glimpses of the obvious; equally I apologise to others who find no explanation for the clues that baffle them. The only advice I can give is that the dictionary will usually help to explain the solution and that the reason why the penny fails to drop is often simpler than the reader imagines.

John Grant
Crossword Editor of *The Times*

# The Puzzles

# 1

**Across**

1 Run skinhead accommodation with some hesitation (7)
5 Pointed to copperhead about to strike first (7)
9 Right – breathe out and relax (5)
10 Dreamy but not solemn composition (9)
11 Has note to mail first, so must be quick (9)
12 Follow directions and engage in litigation (5)
13 Order a little English – Portuguese dictionary (5)
15 Noah kept spinners busy! (9)
18 Called without once getting cocky (9)
19 Finished a cereal food (5)
21 Newsmen in force? (5)
23 Coloured people standing up for William (9)
25 Instruction to rush it may be given quietly (9)
26 Like the heartless Russian leader making a bloomer (5)
27 Hero's love with a sly look about it (7)
28 Note answer in book (7)

**Down**

1 Have misgivings about light-weight (7)
2 A large number come to religious centre for confession (9)
3 Page with a keen desire to chuck it! (5)
4 Defying rates isn't fashionable (9)
5 Hollow business decoration (5)
6 Plant needing little water yet yielding weighty harvest (9)
7 Yards or square measures (5)
8 Movement in net rate leads to appeal (7)
14 Walk about certain to be much appreciated (9)
16 He makes a snatch and turns in smoked fish (9)
17 Organising some great fuel store (9)
18 P for Paris, for instance (7)
20 Place article in box, say (7)
22 At one time craft upside down were spare (5)
23 An article in gold is different (5)
24 Beastly food provided by Greek simpleton (5)

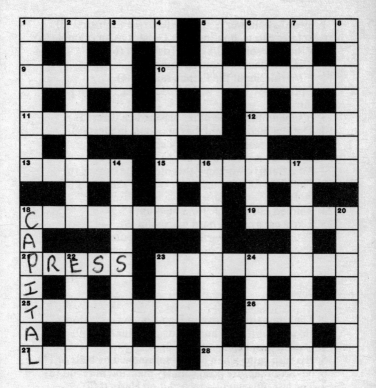

# 2

**Across**

1 Sword-swallower is not one to strike a minstrel (8)
6 Soldier enters, holding back Galatea as an example (6)
9 Visionary sort of fire grips Irish poet (6)
10 Running about following game (8)
11 Firm rule about the French salad (4-4)
12 Optical instrument with head missing but still going (6)
13 It's inaudible to the other players in a team (5)
14 The Colonel, it's said, has one topic in mess (9)
17 Cloth for man at the pottery centre (9)
19 Everyone is after soft fruit (5)
22 An attractive woman – this much one can see (6)
23 The place for pressmen – or women's movement? (4-4)
24 Refined salt suitable for a high-up? (5-3)
25 Like a cat's cradle, hard to explain (6)
26 Caught sight of French art, particoloured (6)
27 They don't usually stand up to the cheese (8)

**Down**

2 The companion I love in Rome is a wild creature (7)
3 He serves little Arthur during drinking bout (9)
4 Gaoled drunken ancient (3-3)
5 His turn came when he was summoned by bells (4,11)
6 No Scots capture posh country mansion in revolt (8)
7 The last judgement – record it on Herbert (7)
8 Canine check (4-5)
13 Collect material for concrete (9)
15 It's not alphabetical, that's obvious, of course (5,4)
16 Having just married Wendy, we left to change (5-3)
18 Perhaps prove to be superior (7)
20 One of the toasts that may be offered with 15 (7)
21 Come to stir (6)

# 3

## Across

1 Bows and scrapes to get marks of approval (12)
8 Opportunity for a trick – put bed behind a tree (7)
9 No entry in the duty-list: he's crowing (7)
11 Wounded lion: the way to warn of the emergency (3,4)
12 Tells of twinges after exercise (7)
13 Free to be at it, that's great (5)
14 Boy comes back to alleviate pet's illness (9)
16 With speed, settler becomes a householder (9)
19 Wait to start play (5)
21 Silly way to carve ham (7)
23 Little craft evident when the boss goes in to bat (3-4)
24 Full-back comes to sort out warm-up (7)
25 Name given to an extremely competitive material (7)
26 By coincidence, a mix-up results in a fatal quarrel (6-6)

## Down

1 Timber man out East becomes a writer (7)
2 Refuse to go through individual cases (7)
3 Recent appointment for judge, we hear (6-3)
4 Football clothes angrily torn off (5)
5 Originally a region lived in by our ancestors (4,3)
6 A sauce boat at a higher price (7)
7 Achievement of the single-minded, not quite mastery? (12)
10 Restoring to life by taking to bed and swallowing the right cure – revolting! (12)
15 Girl ordered her name to go in for the dance (9)
17 Theatrical knight speaking (7)
18 Part company with philosopher – there's no come-uppance (7)
19 It is highly important to change lanes entering M1 (7)
20 Bird colony in Alsatia, for example (7)
22 It has to go in the barn (5)

# 4

**Across**

1 Evidence of a slack washer (4-4)
5 No horns for this composer (6)
8 Phew! drains off in Septimus Harding's office (10)
9 This is blown over border (4)
10 Accepting regime that makes a firm bust (9-5)
11 Muddy lake in outskirts of Salisbury (7)
13 He looks pale in promenade concert (7)
15 Useful part of mission, to discharge worry (7)
18 Tenable variety of May Day celebration (7)
21 Get into the hit parade? (3,3,8)
22 Monkshood, a cure for smoking? (4)
23 Retailer of spicy items (10)
24 Nettle in front of you is close (6)
25 Small pile of sand needs sweeping to get dry (8)

**Down**

1 A little short of words at mess (7)
2 List of people to run Circle Line (9)
3 Running across junction (7)
4 Turn red saying why split up nearly came (7)
5 Induce well-off subject to remember (9)
6 He is still using Veronica in his performance (7)
7 Stop – amber changing to green light (7)
12 Passion over English king's unenlightenment (9)
14 Stern warning from saloon-proprietor at night (4-5)
16 Bearing left in Luton, for example (7)
17 An oil spread in between ends of Lincoln? (7)
18 Money that is found in old golf bag (7)
19 Some rank play by forwards (4-3)
20 Charm of the nineteenth, rallying-point (7)

# 5

**Across**

1 Loose painter? Abandoned (4-3)
5 Wiped floor with woollen fabric (7)
9 Found identical part reversed (5)
10 In agreement? Not I, for one (9)
11 Poison in one's ear – that can be alarming (6)
12 Trace bank for American poet (8)
14 Boxer, for example, has gym equipment (5)
15 Seeing Jack out of job, help (9)
18 It enables one to overlook obstacles (9)
20 Criticism for staff (5)
22 Cuts alternately with one's noble wife (8)
24 Union under Communist control (6)
26 Sort of metal once associated with copper (9)
27 Plants I'd removed from state (5)
28 Seagull seen here? It has wings and flies (7)
29 Buoyant actress (3,4)

**Down**

1 Suit tribunal's member (9)
2 Mixed with cider as cocktail (4-3)
3 For example, first watches veterans (3-6)
4 One's topped by forehead (4)
5 City's victory over another (10)
6 Place to rest up for Joey on the way (5)
7 Terrible strain on a ruler (7)
8 Prevent animal swallowing its tail (5)
13 Practical to double number, and three-quarters? (2-8)
16 Governmental changes prior to New Deal (9)
17 Play a role and break down (4,5)
19 Asian defeat is far from unusual (7)
21 Available to customers, or about to arrive (2,5)
22 He explored Canada initially, with sort of boat (5)
23 Pamphlet followed by pronouncement (5)
25 Bribe to conceal possible source of oil (4)

# 6

**Across**

1 Foreign money I examine found in order (10)
9 Princess with Common Market personal assistant? (6)
10 Momentous as the Olympics, for example (8)
11 What peace-makers try to do is put at risk (8)
12 Notable high-jumper beat it, we hear (4)
13 Main admiral almost wrecked was Hood's friend (4,6)
15 Somehow altered, as deck may be (7)
17 Celebrity's opening switched, as a rule, in Russia (7)
20 Legal document that could be a trap (10)
21 Stylish novel's beginning caught on (4)
23 Settle, or prepare to fight (6,2)
25 Pat his arm in error (8)
26 Philosopher king meant to safeguard property (6)
27 Head off Sheridan's lady, nabbing the same rascal (4-2-4)

**Down**

2 Make merry, taking in a show (6)
3 Lack of employment for lower-class pundit (3-5)
4 Instruct colleague without ceremony (10)
5 Firm hired it for one spell for 7 (4-3)
6 Demand, on the one hand, all the conclusions (4)
7 Flier showing ability in the air line (8)
8 Sort of Tory PM I can name, such as Macmillan (10)
12 Project over the French crew's quarters (10)
14 Plan complex scheme in Michaelmas term? Indeed (10)
16 Brand wild cat spotted below lair (8)
18 Whisk car off in transporter (8)
19 Fire confined to part of church (7)
22 Is king toppled to form republic? (6)
24 Make sound of large vessel (4)

# 7

**Across**

1 In favour of a lock for defence (8)
6 Concerning a very little matter (6)
9 Ornamental cloth discolouring others in the wash? (6)
10 Riding-master moving fitfully against the current (8)
11 Swimmer circling, always restless (8)
12 Take up residence in Ribblesdale (6)
13 Steady and sober, a good man to help (5)
14 Tried on extremely exciting new garment (9)
17 Many an anarchist, corrupt and reckless (9)
19 First appearance of union leader with certain liabilities (5)
22 Curtain material from Communist China? (6)
23 Sound lad with energy – a supporter in emergencies (8)
24 Response to obscurantism? (8)
25 Like the preceding figures, by gum! (6)
26 Teas one's prepared for the rest of the afternoon (6)
27 Harsh head of school I'd put in the river (8)

**Down**

2 Rich man in cipher place (7)
3 Tree's nine great characters (9)
4 Six-footer giving attention to an old politician, say (6)
5 Hants resort's estates include one in the Pacific (5,3,7)
6 Two creatures at home to John Wilkes Booth (8)
7 A great conductor rates badly in Missouri (7)
8 Able to force student to leave temporary accommodation (9)
13 Border poet with whiskers (9)
15 Old, and such a loon, was the Mariner (4-5)
16 Some cooking fashionable among the French? (8)
18 Fury about current measure leads to violent behaviour (7)
20 After University, leading Scotsman becomes an idealist (7)
21 A fellow above-board in business (6)

# 8

## Across

1 Provided in turn, in vessels, hot and cold food (4,3,5)
8 A show of boldness provides support against trouble (7)
9 Wind round about after battle (7)
11 Arrange deposit for part of ship (7)
12 Trivial greeting in Cornwall, say (7)
13 'Right you are!' say nearly all of the country (5)
14 Fish are involved with the main current (2,3,4)
16 'Not usually rent-free' I butt in (9)
19 Cove's home rented (5)
21 Tramps let Barnaby in the back way (7)
23 He may give a seat to someone standing (7)
24 One fare carried amongst additional part of Masefield's cargoes (7)
25 Dormant state – 18 are in it (7)
26 Hurry, then stop, ordered retired pundit (4,2,3,3)

## Down

1 Stew for each girl (7)
2 Dog that's left to follow oxen (7)
3 Together once (2,3,4)
4 Maud's developed into a writer (5)
5 Man given, note, an extremely (in its earliest stage) poisonous plant (7)
6 It provided for the needy prisoner to receive gold, accompanied by a note (4,3)
7 Passing comment, ring loafer about prohibition, omitting name (6,6)
10 We stammer and get confused in Manhattan (3,9)
15 Cast without English find it hard immediately (9)
17 Traveller, a gentleman, is up in everything foreign (7)
18 Reorganise soldiers attached to division (7)
19 I see, so to speak, a diving bird coming up – a marine hazard (7)
20 Understatement apparent in stories about drink (7)
22 Showing resolve, we left at start of film (5)

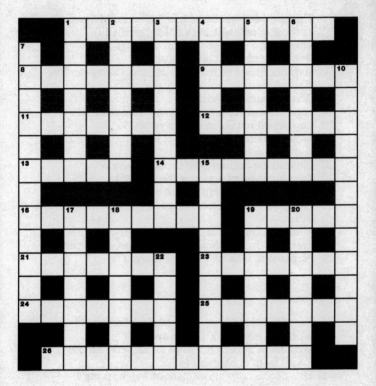

**Across**

1 Fish and wine served with inclusive supplement (7)
5 Exalted, as was Mikado's object, totally (7)
9 Brought low since getting into debt (5)
10 Happen to change course (4,5)
11 Style embraced by the Spanish for covering canines (6)
12 Horatius could be back (8)
14 Legitimate student expelled with dire result (5)
15 Competent to take in a river vessel (9)
18 Joint study perhaps indicates scope for expansion (5-4)
20 Close to the beginning of the darkness (5)
22 Telephone out of action is the limit (8)
24 State vehicle found in Italian resort (6)
26 The good old days recollected in Donegal, for example (6,3)
27 Abundant ingredient of cream – plenty of it (5)
28 Entertain doubts about assistant to police inquiry (7)
29 Prepared to wait for doctor's charge (7)

**Down**

1 Event of course descriptive of Houyhnhnms (5-4)
2 Women's work for girl employees (7)
3 Member of Society not even an academician (9)
4 Recoil from excitement (4)
5 This necessitates adjustment of watch spring's follower (6,4)
6 Second-class track event or two (5)
7 Tidy as monks are (2,5)
8 Participate in record (5)
13 Relation supported by worker engaged in finance (10)
16 Beggar will make something good out of tin (9)
17 Poor men turn it into foodstuff (9)
19 Fliers subscribe to a follower of hounds (7)
21 Catch sight of proceeds irregularly taken in notes (7)
22 Note kind of brush taken up by Impressionist (5)
23 Owing loyalty to a Belgian community (5)
25 Harvest pear damaged (4)

# 10

**Across**

1 Metal from beasts wild and woolly (7)
5 For whom a headline may help to make a fortune? (7)
9 One's out of place under news chief, getting sacked (9)
10 Printed material initially all together included in small book (5)
11 Hearing noisy neighbour could be one (5)
12 Flowering shrub to give cover to forest officer, say (9)
14 Thomas gets par again – extraordinary show of illusion (14)
17 Those detailed by Mrs Giles (5,5,4)
21 In this forum other witnesses show common sense (6,3)
23 One in real trouble freed by the Duke of Milan (5)
24 She shows originally slender young lines – perfectly heavenly (5)
25 Clever chap swallows a tot perhaps going to Dover in this (4-5)
26 Concerning duplicated functions of the screen (7)
27 Bound to finish, following directions (7)

**Down**

1 Deer seen in an excavation in Mayfair (6)
2 Pupil on strike is hard, rough and uncouth (7)
3 Air of fragrance or colour once embracing the French style (9)
4 Sweet product of the wet land, many admit (11)
5 Lodging for an old-time horse (3)
6 Sign for much of the book collection (5)
7 Get in trouble about coming up with a figure (7)
8 Reaction of Hoffmann's Augustus to the soup from this restaurant? (4-4)
13 Show way to chide the devil on top (11)
15 Such exercises ruined my casting (9)
16 Spray given first of all to Scrooge (8)
18 A very fine type of snake (7)
19 Elegance given a trial in Illinois (7)
20 Some swimmers take this breather during physical education (6)

22  Hoped for a change of vestment (5)
25  A kiss, say, which may transport one (3)

# 11

**Across**

1 Demonstration of professional taking the lead (5)
4 Emperor recently arrived with Scot (9)
9 Heat burns silly baker (9)
10 Old hat taken out by American (5)
11 Period in which no striker's caught in slips (6)
12 Are the cars he heads off to go through? (8)
14 Rank and file radicals are on to informer (5,5)
16 Substance found in mine's hard (4)
19 Stretcher cases may be put on one (4)
20 Reduced in price, fair or inferior in quality (4-6)
22 Wild Etruscan horsemen (8)
23 Amazement as bloody present's returned (6)
26 Unsuitable French friendship (5)
27 Money-belt for these musicians (5,4)
28 No female runners in this park? (9)
29 The French king's about to unwind (5)

**Down**

1 Weak team member transferred by coach, perhaps (9)
2 One who has new order accepted by other ranks (5)
3 Note match that's as even as possible (8)
4 British painter, such as Constable (4)
5 Mineral water in London (10)
6 Certainly at home with legal document (6)
7 Join together to carry out burial with torch (9)
8 Gentle push exposed key hidden inside (5)
13 Trusty Jack, perhaps, a sort of seaman (10)
15 Result of upward mobility in British Isle? (9)
17 Dissident foolishly rings the Red Cross (9)
18 Merry-maker's driver imbibing nothing (8)
21 Service provided in the Peak District (6)
22 Spelling in Daily Mirror's leader (5)
24 In a manner of speaking, slowly extract pound (5)
25 Soundly tarred? That's settled (4)

# 12

**Across**

1 Married woman is 19 (6)
4 Weaken when police come back in, and give up (8)
10 Terminated without a messy injury (9)
11 Bird call caught by chance (5)
12 Foreigner said to come first at university examination (5-2)
13 It makes me a lord (7)
14 Ruled and guided without having been elected (5)
15 Gopher wood used for it – northern hardwood with spots about in it (5,3)
18 Landlord breaks silence before the last of the ale (8)
20 A lot of shops can have almost incredible novelties when they first open (5)
23 Ruler taking a bit of fruit (7)
25 On the whole, it provides protection (7)
26 Foreign national I encountered therein (5)
27 Brush blue carpet (5,4)
28 Longing to swallow the drink lying around, but procrastinating (8)
29 Produced a harsh sound, the band, for an audience (6)

**Down**

1 12's in charge, wearing decorations (8)
2 Helping you to forget three articles (not all in English) (7)
3 American titmouse, a little bird ending with a D (9)
5 Monkey that bees disturbed, similarly (2,3,4,5)
6 Run into fashionable cowardly fellow (5)
7 For instance, lower rent (7)
8 Dane, perhaps, reads Kipling's book in English as well (6)
9 In holds I submit, to stay in practice (4,4,4,2)
16 It follows when crocuses are treated with sulphur (9)
17 Tending to be incorporated with 14 (8)
19 I shall leave behind hard feelings (3,4)
21 True-blue's claim about love (7)
22 One's left with a key (6)
24 Get some round number (5)

## 12

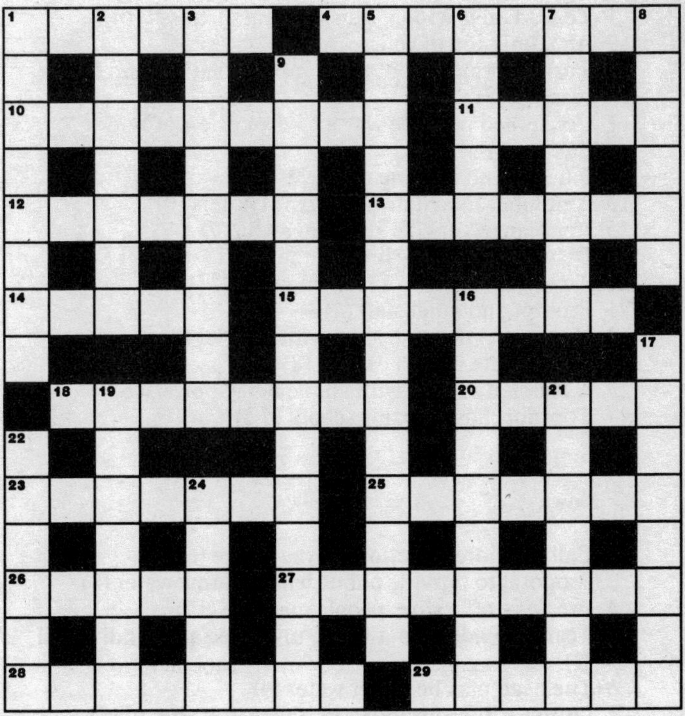

# 13

**Across**

1 To lead on is wrong, causing great distress (10)
9 An admission of course (6)
10 Turn informer about the company that's found to be twisting (8)
11 Concerned with the way a foreign priest provides therapy (4-4)
12 Fare offered in some nurseries (4)
13 A number to irritate a woman? Quite! (10)
15 Vengeance, making sin seem awful (7)
17 Disturbed by a few lines in the Old Testament (7)
20 American beggar – a kitchen worker? (10)
21 Prompt and quiet staff (4)
23 Non-professional dealing with an idler (8)
25 Esteem rate reform certain (8)
26 A Russian vehicle with ample horse-power! (6)
27 Tops for those starting school (5,5)

**Down**

2 Call for more directions to the centre (6)
3 Proposal to provide public with running water (8)
4 Breaking off a story people make up (10)
5 Tearing madly about for an unappreciative individual (7)
6 The head may be under water (4)
7 Drinks will be provided for the men on board (8)
8 Outraged, though that may be dead secret (10)
12 Mark one turning up at the last minute for work (10)
14 'For forms of — let fools contest' (Pope) (10)
16 This offers potential savers an opening (5-3)
18 Genuine acceptance of publicity is giving satisfaction (8)
19 After midnight youngsters sparkle (7)
22 Big bloomer made by a revered figure in ancient Egypt (6)
24 A Scandinavian writing of taking in the French (4)

# 14

**Across**

1 Supporter of a hanger-on, it's plain, needs to be end-lessly wealthy (7)
5 Set in lake, on the bed (7)
9 Secured work – embarrassed about it (5)
10 May it hold together extract from dissertation? (5-4)
11 Physicist's team with sound advantage in the scrum? (9)
12 Material progress suddenly made, we hear (5)
13 Lowest point in N. Adirondacks (5)
15 Charges from Friendly Society (9)
18 Compulsion to fire one man, or pay badly (9)
19 Bitch's principle? (5)
21 Huge tin of tongue forgotten (5)
23 Cobbler's farewell ceremony? (4,5)
25 No exclusive way of communicating 19 (5,4)
26 About to help name a girl (5)
27 Take once more the road to Tyre (7)
28 After end of visit, lock up the abbey (7)

**Down**

1 The stream outside used to be a nuisance (7)
2 Northerner concealed proposal in two foreign articles (9)
3 More than one spoke of operating limits (5)
4 Island with food for goat (9)
5 Police chase ending in the wood (5)
6 Beat long-established minimum value (9)
7 Chief mourner accepts a pound (5)
8 Train to be articulate (7)
14 Part with money, curious to discover the way in which these clues are set (5,4)
16 RIP to a rag-doll, we hear (9)
17 When it's dark the moon's plain; or is that a fantasy? (9)
18 Correct to hold son is to succeed (7)
20 Refuse to vote, putting Jack on the spot (7)
22 Apprentice leaves the wine; it shows there's some-thing lacking (5)

14

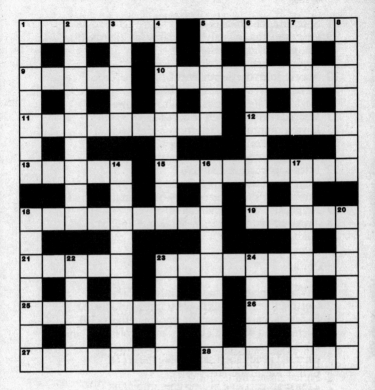

23 One fat round Scotsman (5)
24 He chiselled the staff, when elected (5)

35

# 15

**Across**

1 Spies hidden office (6,7)
9 One prepared to analyse anybody in title role (9)
10 The state of penal reform (5)
11 Bag's become wrinkled (5)
12 Accent from the South-West? (4)
13 28 includes two of this crew (4)
15 Regularly late? Sounds chivalrous, however (7)
17 Injured fliers returned to base (7)
18 Upstart out of place in group is architect (7)
20 Twist head off each vegetable (7)
21 First river out of line? European one (4)
22 Miss a sporting occasion (4)
23 Religious leader unlikely to be elder (5)
26 Score team's opening century, in dramatic form (5)
27 Emphasise it's less than 14 (9)
28 Two-and-six, perhaps, in old money (6,2,5)

**Down**

1 Favourite place for having tantrums? (8-6)
2 Getting this increases don's standing, oddly (5)
3 For instance, new concerti ignoring others (10)
4 Such a good type isn't commonly involved in cunning (7)
5 Channel needs good sailors like these (7)
6 Centre for missionaries (4)
7 Transport carrying bishop goes into plant (9)
8 Mad Hatter fled rage king displayed (6,3,5)
14 Chart showing relative positions (6,4)
16 Bird set out on part of flight in March (5,4)
19 Country divided by Trade Union legislation (7)
20 Broadcast – and needle, we hear, unnamed person (2-3-2)
24 What's employer doing to make union leader whistle? (5)
25 Mule, for example – soundly beat it! (4)

# 16

### Across

1 One much-loved tale reworked: *The King and I* (5,3)
5 Old player's son good at cricket practice (6)
10 Some tomatoes to prepare for the oven (5)
11 Supplier dismissed – successor is more suitable (9)
12 Small girl is sensible to be frugal (5,4)
13 Stop officer functioning (5)
14 Lecture on fairy's transformation (7)
16 Vice yields record-breaking tax (6)
19 Eye of day – after a fight? (6)
21 Sort of underwear for the officer cadet? (7)
23 Uncle who helped found city (5)
25 Sort of pastel colour laid on thick (9)
27 Old Emperor's wife puts man in strait-jacket (9)
28 A dead bird is (5)
29 Cupid, say, brings a sort of light to a girl (6)
30 Moll's field (8)

### Down

1 French triple crown claimant has a new piece of advice : take no exercise (8)
2 A good hand for what's top of the charts (4,5)
3 Uncertain, but state where pie may be (5)
4 Fertile crescent (7)
6 Rule the Head enunciated (9)
7 Concerning arrival in South Africa (5)
8 Small boy put in the high chair (6)
9 Frequent chaperon (6)
15 Take circuitous route on climb near Lake District once (9)
17 Less violent way to be a conqueror (9)
18 Finish up having a drink outside for pleasure (8)
20 Salesman to publicise condition of goods (6)
21 The path to encompass a victory for Labour (7)
22 Villainous deed on a battle-ground (6)
24 Permanent accompaniment to fine Banbury lady (5)
26 Exercise sequence (5)

*This puzzle was solved within 30 minutes by 11 per cent of the competitors at the 1988 Birmingham regional final of The Times Collins Dictionaries Crossword Championship.*

# 17

## Across

1 Whisky for Alfonso XIII, for one (7)
5 Cavalryman and strolling player, by the sound of it (7)
9 Musicians, etc., represented in Holy Writ (5)
10 Gradual reduction of the figure essential for astronauts (5-4)
11 Followed closely, being obstinately determined (6)
12 Antiquated – therefore permitted to be held in honour (8)
14 Classically elegant, such a story (5)
15 Odd device for converting motion (9)
18 Not a striking example of the horologist's craft (9)
20 This man may be fed in the target area (5)
22 It can yet conceal firmness of purpose (8)
24 One demonstrating a bathroom appliance (6)
26 Gloomy spell in South Africa, and in the East (9)
27 Mountain nymph who wore a diadem inside (5)
28 Lawless extremists in Rio, perhaps, cut from 25 (7)
29 Anticipate a lower-stream class, say (7)

## Down

1 Programme includes somewhat coarse actors (9)
2 At university, tense and angry (7)
3 Flatter about a hundred in the plant (9)
4 Hard to abandon the recess – it's so agreeable (4)
5 With which to torture little Tom's lot! (10)
6 Go one better than an alfresco party? (5)
7 Original explorer – one embraced by Mole (7)
8 Row in the kitchen (5)
13 Uninspired footman (10)
16 Boring hue disguising one close to us (9)
17 This paper found in a magazine? (9)
19 Observe and record activity of the Komodo dragon (7)
21 Modern look of headquarters? Just the opposite (7)
22 Good man upset about request for assignments (5)
23 Collector's item we find strange? Not us (5)
25 Complaint from egghead among Gort's men (4)

# 17

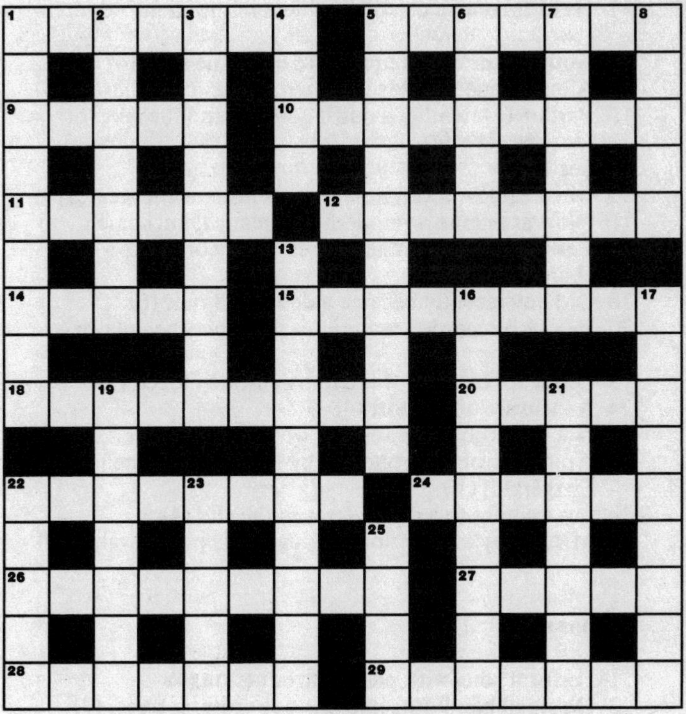

# 18

**Across**

1 Head takes in a classical subject in the count's domain (10)
6 Authentication is required to enter the state (4)
9 After 25 queen holds it the wrong way (very hard) (10)
10 Part of 12-member's outfit going round the lake (or loch, rather?) (4)
12 See 10 (4)
13 One headless form, human, this instrument creates (9)
15 Old war engine or modern aeroplane launcher (8)
16 Tea round the chimney retreat that works like a charm (6)
18 Old boy recently became a dedicated type (6)
20 In which recorded material is fixed between players, say (8)
23 Glum appearance of the fourth estate indeed (9)
24 A measure of old port (4)
26 Not one who begat Joshua, we hear (4)
27 'Spitting from lips once — by Hers' (Browning to Fitzgerald) (10)
28 Love comes to a pachyderm in the end (4)
29 Mistake by master floundering in the pilot's wake (10)

**Down**

1 Perform song with piano introduction (4)
2 Do small hand-outs like this one grow on trees? (7)
3 Job for a Dickensian going round Spain perhaps, checking rail transport (5-7)
4 Where wicked madmen go? Must be crackers to break into it (8)
5 Doctor catches fish in arctic region? Quite the reverse (6)
7 First thing to do to an alteration (7)
8 Martin Tate contrived to make this hypothetical stuff (10)
11 Former Soviet minister, one at the food supply department (12)

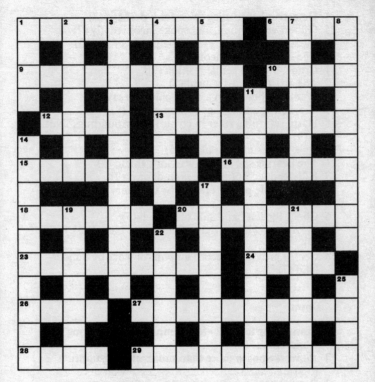

14 Bill, with French horn, is on the ball, showing conformity (10)
17 Could the rat race be called, like Kipling's book, life's —? (8)
19 Naval battle for the French Christmas show (7)
21 Call it the end of the wood destroyer (7)
22 Attack makes Balaam's mount unwell (6)
25 Gardener with a beastly mother? He had 26 (4)

# 19

1 Detective has to stick to Oxford, perhaps (7)
5 Gilbert was injured, and spoke incoherently (7)
9 I was tired, to some extent, being out of bed (5)
10 The way to carry bacon? (9)
11 Crude, but in a gentle fashion (9)
12 The artist Edward valued (5)
13 Went in a boat or in a car, would you say? (5)
15 'ibernating animal has to stop in city (9)
18 Harm returning ruler in colourful surroundings? Not I! (9)
19 One, for instance, is like it (5)
21 The bearing shown in a warrior's shield (5)
23 Kill dead, accepting one pound for it (9)
25 Remarkable people created by O. Henry (pen name) (9)
26 Check the left hand side of the hall (5)
27 Messenger with no right of entry into New York house (7)
28 Centre providing record amount of work by Sunderland (7)

**Down**

1 Less willing to work after completion of building, workman . . . (7)
2 . . . worked with more than rudimentary gumption (6,3)
3 Drove to store, by the sound of it (5)
4 For a walk, East European goes round the mountains, climbing (9)
5 Progress, in some degree, for a zealot (5)
6 Date of Derby in doubt (3-6)
7 Inclined to sound fast (5)
8 Landing-craft leaves Wales on the way up to Edinburgh, perhaps (7)
14 Sported in storm, it keeps the rain off (9)
16 A triangle put on top of another figure (3,6)
17 Cannibalism, with no holds barred (3-3-3)

18 About mechanisation of clerical work, cleric is poker-
   faced (4,3)
20 In America they reverse the ending of this dramatic
   art (7)
22 Environmentalist has not smoked (5)
23 Knowing there's shelter over the line (5)
24 Empty hotel without a natural base (5)

# 20

**Across**

1 Chopped pear in fresh soft cheese (10)
6 Mild, perhaps, this part of Devon (4)
10 Saw dog's name inside lead (7)
11 Unvarying habit? (7)
12 Learn about Toad's accident in main lay-by (9)
13 Some trees of Israel emit this fragrant resin (5)
14 Coming before a superior (5)
15 Game target of a river authority (9)
17 Hurricane, for example, engulfs soldiers in cargo-ship (9)
20 Line right for a fast cycle? (5)
21 Texan mission fashionable, mostly (5)
23 Contents of *The Old Curiosity Shop* translated into French (4-1-4)
25 Monied sort caught like one possessed (7)
26 East Judaean procurator to remove sideboards (7)
27 Routine hospital meeting for this girl (4)
28 He was in a rush to strike in America (5-5)

**Down**

1 Spring shrub (5)
2 Summoning up energy to take a dressing case, say (9)
3 Fair location for gladness on earth (8-6)
4 Multiply without going forth? (7)
5 Illegally transfer money in Arundel exchange (7)
7 Run off irregularly with sweetheart (5)
8 Jogger admits a rest is needed here (9)
9 I'm in skateboard mishap coming down gangway (14)
14 Inflation could make this a dangerous summer (4-5)
16 Cartesian formula to learn surely (9)
18 Robert Burton's superexcellent drawing material? (7)
19 Clothing design torn outside (7)
22 Own commercial with foreign support (5)
24 Make a profit with no trouble (5)

# 21

**Across**

1 It denotes the rank of some military band (6)
4 A graduate cut yet poised (8)
10 It's quite true about weapons changing (7)
11 Sporting individuals who never look where they're going (7)
12 Assembly, part male in composition (10)
13 Germanic invader well-known for sacking! (4)
15 Service book number (7)
17 Beg leaderless men to negotiate (7)
19 Woolly-minded joiner? (7)
21 Great hotel in a European city (7)
23 A slap on the wrist? (4)
24 'All that is human must — if it does not advance' (Gibbon) (10)
27 Belgian broadcast in a foreign language (7)
28 Copper is at home with Oriental cookery (7)
29 Readiness to allow a little credit among non-professional people (8)
30 Game put in nets maybe (6)

**Down**

1 Discard reserve cuttings? (5-4)
2 Greatly honoured, though always getting into debt (7)
3 Eager to hand one over with a note (10)
5 Sadly mend a torn decoration (9)
6 The vibes of gunmen after gold (4)
7 Appear to include set work out (7)
8 In a small garden seedlings have to be close-planted (5)
9 Apprentice breaking open river shellfish (4)
14 A prison-camp child growing up (10)
16 The criminal's alternative isn't clear (9)
18 There's some strain when the head gets under ten points (9)
20 The princess's baby with a following (7)
22 Object over a pin-up that's not British (7)
23 Snake and swan painter (5)

25  Course for an ethnic group (4)
26  Piano music – a duet (4)

**Across**

1 Part Belloc used to play in this place (5)
4 Bottoms as seen in night club entertainment (5,4)
9 Cracking the French Barmaid mystery (9)
10 Walrus is further round the bend (5)
11 Sturdy flower, first of the year (6)
12 Prior and clergyman in religious surroundings (8)
14 Big trouble about angry writer (5,5)
16 Dance circle lost member (4)
19 There may be a charge for these fish (4)
20 Stress – a point with worn foundations (10)
22 Mere existence? (4-4)
23 What you'd expect of a chimp – a moped crash (6)
26 Celebrated without wife, and got suspended! (5)
27 Badly cut, perhaps, when chasing a thug (5-4)
28 Playfellows square the law (9)
29 Pique shown by a novice? That's a bit of a bloomer (5)

**Down**

1 A lot take an accent to be something attractive (9)
2 Turned up with duck in relief – it's carved (5)
3 The batsmen out (8)
4 Watch pockets – cheats appearing (4)
5 Bowling dominated and made ineffective (10)
6 A form of transport (6)
7 How Winnie might be described educationally (9)
8 Considers small points (5)
13 It is played in panto – that is, for funny parts (10)
15 Left the close wearing woman's head-dress with a
   marigold (9)
17 Having two names gives Mark no new alibi, unfortu-
   nately (9)
18 Police dance – just the place for ready-mades (4-4)
21 Engagement is in a mess (6)
22 Beat with stick (5)
24 Spoke at length – for many, a heavy blow (5)
25 Elephantine frenzy from new wine (4)

*This puzzle was solved within 30 minutes by 7 per cent of the competitors at the 1988 Birmingham regional final of The Times Collins Dictionaries Crossword Championship.*

# 23

**Across**

1 Boatman in part of the island (6)
5 'Speech created thought, which is the measure of the
   —' (Shelley) (8)
9 Like one treating Ida with scorn (8)
10 Quick to help players (6)
11 Happened to be on the ground (8)
12 Publican with no end of trade (6)
13 Dismissed side entirely (8)
15 Cliff, mark . . . (4)
17 . . . was an explorer, by the way (4)
19 In balance, for instance, one with a means of recogni-
   tion (8)
20 'ow to beat one's wife, say, at this game? (6)
21 Cures, with prohibition of careless play (8)
22 Scold worker about to desert (6)
23 Bond uses decoy to surround one gun (8)
24 Refinement can perhaps appear in a threnody (8)
25 Worn the other way round by Labour man in rows?
   (6)

**Down**

2 Of purely theoretical interest to the professor (8)
3 It hots things up in the cooler (8)
4 Wearing a vest – one in a suit (9)
5 International body and state combine, with no strings
   (15)
6 Sport five song books (7)
7 Distantly provide accommodation in Rye perhaps (8)
8 Obtained by force out of wrong pressman (8)
14 Farmworker having the sense to be wise with this (9)
15 Was not Macbeth's dagger, he asked, — to feeling as
   to sight? (8)
16 A claret with a new sort of menu (1,2,5)
17 Clasp made by better artist (8)

18  Soldiers lead when, for example, others get up and
come out again (2-6)
19  A tendency not to move in rate revision without one
(7)

# 24

**Across**

1 Caught in the act, describing Ulster's badge (3-6)
6 Wine – its lack may cause domestic upheaval (5)
9 Criticise war-time legislation as the source of many ills (7)
10 Festive occasion round here abroad in Spain (7)
11 A single withered French flower (5)
12 I get a rule changed by the local Nazi boss (9)
13 Fixes directions at the end of a page (8)
15 What's the matter about money? It's an advantage (4)
19 Had a terrible time getting fruit from this (4)
20 Boss given a turn by the new arrival (8)
23 Idle learner sure to be confounded without this calculator (5-4)
24 Sunbathed, topless, as requested (5)
26 Slatternly type of Barset chronicler, we hear (7)
27 With endless work advanced to become rich (7)
28 So smart a guy, Bumppo the deerslayer (5)
29 Jack Ketch's attachment to hosiery (9)

**Down**

1 Put material on edge and tear a strip off (9)
2 Stupid fellow caught hiding in a sand-hill (5)
3 Lack of capital cover by oil organisation inter alia (8)
4 Game that may give one a cold? (8)
5 Canoe of superannuated type back in service (3-3)
6 Pound metal roughly with a hammer (6)
7 Hamlet's fell sergeant includes many over fifty on this sporting contest (9)
8 Academic appointment taken by the president (5)
14 Lane describing type of government (9)
16 Getting out of bed, one seeking engagement as a journalist (3-6)
17 Firm on prohibition, America is breaking a commandment (8)
18 Rising artist, fully developed, is a bit of a dynamo (8)
21 Mix-up when grassland is covered by the sea (6)
22 Commotion caused by the odd Manx cat (6)

23 Material that fetches money in Cape Town (5)
25 Say, want to make some dough? (5)

# 25

**Across**

1 London road, en route from Exeter to Lincoln (6,6)
9 Did judge get times wrong – date also? (9)
10 Faction to carry on rising without ring-leader (5)
11 Slight trauma for doctor (6)
12 Certain you'll get this from crack shot (4-4)
13 Grandmaster's opening with added scope? (6)
15 Careless mistakes brick-carrier can make (8)
18 Sort of licence required for cart, is it? (8)
19 Other team member initially in good shape for county (6)
21 Flower one found on short walk (8)
23 Persian singer gets male almost beside himself (6)
26 Key locks piece of furniture (5)
27 Fish cooked in lard – chips, too (9)
28 It's not popular, as a rule (12)

**Down**

1 Moves at first opportunity (7)
2 Lots of fast news, with odd bits missing (5)
3 I'm held up by exchanges of shots in battle (9)
4 One of the first people named in Somerset House (4)
5 Foreign money Edward put in to show confidence in contract (8)
6 Sort of score that demands perfect pitch? (5)
7 Point captured by European side – one finishing top of table (8)
8 Insert pages in a final section? (6)
14 Stuff that's relevant (8)
16 Writer, as opposed to drawer with pencil? (9)
17 State of short race described in novel (8)
18 To criticise like this can be offensive (6)
20 Male type so quiet he's feeble (7)
22 Inn – the main one around the river (5)
24 Flog what might be silver (5)
25 Accidental result of nail on road? (4)

# 26

**Across**

1 Weep and wail, say, to a large extent (7)
5 Improved, having swotted (7)
9 No use leaving caged bird inside (5)
10 Brilliant star's marvellous Avon come-back (9)
11 Sort of niche right for ornament (6)
12 Brave a terribly long family line (8)
14 Champion gunners win back the palm (5)
15 Grey horse named Merry Monarch (3,6)
18 In the lattice is a stained glass window (9)
20 Time to go down to Kew, said Noyes (5)
22 Spirit of ancient Greek town attracting artist after artist (8)
24 Enthusiastic devotee did act badly (6)
26 Old British supremo writing to keeper of the treasury (9)
27 Where the towers, being topless, got burnt in Marlowe (5)
28 He annoys the king with record-player (7)
29 He takes a toll with his spearhead (7)

**Down**

1 A negro mob in disorder returning missile (9)
2 Rapid rise of swell at college (7)
3 A comforter in battle (9)
4 Wine increased in strength (4)
5 Steps taken when a vessel needs scaling (4-6)
6 Maiden has the right spirit (5)
7 The tube for below-surface travel (7)
8 Row about Arsenal and drink (5)
13 Morgan's sign gets jovial acknowledgment (5,5)
16 Drunken counsel rejects water (5,4)
17 Sailor may scan the endless rocks (9)
19 Huge individual gets medal on points (7)
21 The state of the people is calm, I hazard (7)
22 Literary figure first detected in the Rue Morgue (5)

23 We hear you're articled in the middle of the country
(5)
25 Bargain for crop (4)

# 27

**Across**

1 Excitement as tension explodes (9)
6 Being amusing, it dispels gloom (5)
9 About to cut a prison stretch (7)
10 Check, blow up, and fire a lot (7)
11 A Belgian university subject (5)
12 Given tranquillisers, a bull in a frenzy lies captured (9)
13 The diversion of profits (8)
15 A highlight of the night that's clear (4)
19 Romance found in retirement in Israel (4)
20 A sign of distress brings rent reduction (8)
23 Talk the underworld way (9)
24 Humble woman embracing a Mohammedan initially (5)
26 Pole, having to fly, packing (7)
27 A people backing one could be a bloomer (7)
28 It's an odd sort of stuff (5)
29 Patient attention expected from 2 *dn* (9)

**Down**

1 Working steam-mill of no great importance (5-4)
2 She tends to rush over certain points (5)
3 'Hell is full of musical —: music is the brandy of the damned' (Shaw) (8)
4 Thought the holy man about 51 a visionary (8)
5 A head with totally unsatisfactory delivery (2-4)
6 God against Russell's view of ghosts (6)
7 Trial – a dog's involved, a fighter (9)
8 Some actresses do their own hair (5)
14 Convey delight (9)
16 Substitute for military personnel now (9)
17 Refuse to put a philosopher in jug? Quite the reverse! (8)
18 The outlook for a class of people going about quietly (8)
21 A moving proposal (6)
22 Clever bishop, on the conservative side (6)

23 Bearing in some animals, administers medication (5)
25 A sound opener to admire (5)

# 28

**Across**

1 Leading actor honoured – a formality (6)
4 Friendly note in a message (8)
10 This garment a favourite with Cato? It could be (9)
11 Jargon used by many in turn (5)
12 Former spouse with right to make an outcry? (7)
13 Old journeyman's story (7)
14 In logic he lacked a disciple (5)
15 Work as guide in Ulster, causing a confrontation (4-4)
18 See Birkenhead shiver convulsively – he's so ill (8)
20 Sail back with ring and aristocratic jewel (5)
23 Rejected outcry about state's prevarication (7)
25 What the unscrupulous stop at in bagatelle (7)
26 First question put by republicans to an Arab (5)
27 Dinosaur's droppings in one river (9)
28 One expects quarrels in this dramatist's work (8)
29 Girl with fish to sell down the river (6)

**Down**

1 Wisdom I discovered in South American coppers (8)
2 Object to topping part of speech (7)
3 A new chair adapted for the use of diners (9)
5 Union attendant holding up a train (6,2,6)
6 Company of soldiers swallow the foreign fish (5)
7 It has endless teeth, as musicians discovered (4-3)
8 Poe's characters? Shakespeare's corporal? Little
   Dorrit, for one (6)
9 Cinema attendant gets percentage on *The Sound Of
   Music* (14)
16 Society girl's television rise? A poet's written about it
   (9)
17 Wine, or posh food, upset daughter in New York (8)
19 Issue half of them – a neat arrangement (7)
21 Little woman in the German legal union (7)
22 An outstanding replacement for old watch (6)
24 Initially it's lost if anyone cuts this artery (5)

*This puzzle was solved within 30 minutes by 24 per cent of the competitors at the 1988 Leeds regional final of The Times Collins Dictionaries Crossword Championship.*

# 29

**Across**

1 High-level support – it's raised boisterously by old actor (4-4)
5 After drink, extremely lazy and fat (6)
8 Cliché of a hi-fi buff? (10)
9 Get rid of Falstaff's tipple (4)
10 It may provide soldiers' livelihood (5,3,6)
11 Encyclopaedist – was 'e left to languish? (7)
13 Point to observe about international runner (7)
15 Dead beat, and sadly they're behind the main body (7)
18 Stand up and present difficulties (7)
21 Opening some sauce and masking what's bad (6-8)
22 Find fault with apple (4)
23 Search in police precinct gets a supplier of narcotics (10)
24 Organ known for its spitefulness (6)
25 Copied character of the Greeks, high-spirited on the outside (8)

**Down**

1 Appeared to start growing into a lovely girl (4-3)
2 Went in first without result, there being no boundaries (4-5)
3 One crushing point admitted by merchant (7)
4 No longer active, divorcée can put on weight (7)
5 John the Baptist, for example – sprucer or more unkempt? (9)
6 Arose in agony, dry inside as a stone (7)
7 Cattle feed in the lake (7)
12 Did Goldfinger give casual work to this chap? (3-6)
14 A slip, trivial-sounding, over some paint (9)
16 Bit of moisture removed finally by spreading powder (7)
17 Make someone barren, it's said, and send to another place (7)
18 Lack of interest of left-winger in improving economic conditions (7)

19  This month, everyone is to get ready to work (7)
20  Defile and glen in the country (7)

**Across**

1 Nearest point at sea for the launch (12)
9 Scheme for chum to embrace another from Bow (9)
10 Something pronounced in shorter English dictionary (5)
11 Working order of Scottish outfitter, say? (6)
12 Spear tempered, it takes a year for this sharpness (8)
13 Bareness of recent simple song heard (6)
15 Summary court-martial where tattoo takes place (8)
18 Blue, perhaps, at university who never gets a first (6-2)
19 Lupin-raiser, this Holloway journalist (6)
21 Pop ethics adapted for musical medley (8)
23 Clan leader is in tartan still (6)
26 Incentives for footballers (5)
27 Girl has an awful trip to this place in the Himalayas (7-2)
28 Well, in Italy, loud tragedienne can be an angel (12)

**Down**

1 Persistently ask the family for fruit (7)
2 Top forty, as the Romans said (5)
3 Where the ground-rent is most severe? (9)
4 Duck leaves lake (4)
5 Exchange rate certain to bring riches (8)
6 Daisy is a neat looker (2-3)
7 Embrocation of mine spread inside surgical dressing (8)
8 Remained sober, you say? (6)
14 This reptile is around no longer (8)
16 Hooch sonata? (9)
17 Way to serve potatoes, just stuffed with game (8)
18 Pop in what's left for a meal (6)
20 MPs who intervene in Service quarrels (7)
22 Controversy in broadcast topic (5)
24 Scold veiled in church (5)
25 Fun for students with a note-system in India (4)

# 30

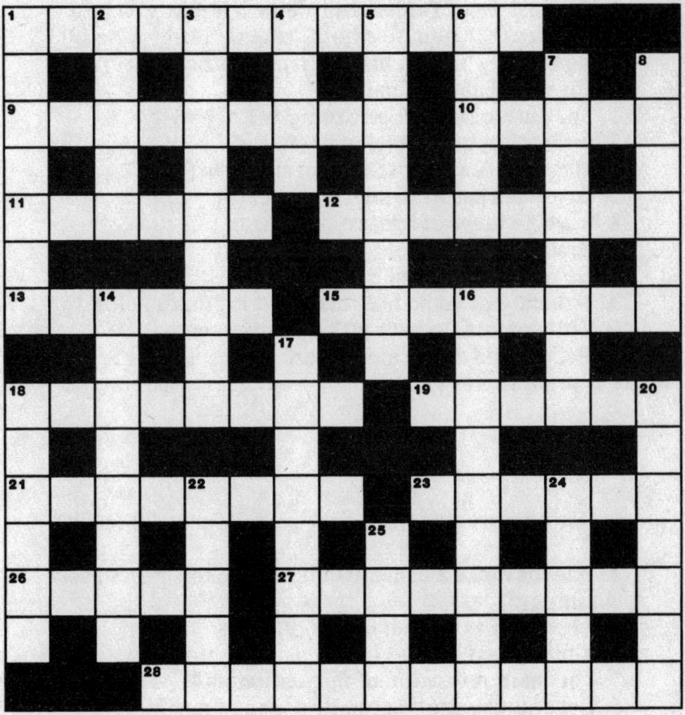

# 31

**Across**

1 Translation of Dumas and Verne – it may well be a disaster (12)
9 Where he who uses his ears reaps the benefit (9)
10 Speak evil about none (5)
11 The author of 'Golden Spring' (6)
12 Birds without recent equals (8)
13 Magical 4 – a river to inspire affection (6)
15 Force journalists to stick to water (8)
18 A whole range of light colours (8)
19 Grab a few notes (6)
21 Go on about say one caught in a dreadful deed (8)
23 Trouble caused by holy man interrupting a fellow (6)
26 Left a painter to back go slow movement (5)
27 Get out and create aid to work (9)
28 People at play (7-5)

**Down**

1 Little beasts steal inside, the cause of some ill-feeling (7)
2 One may take a drink with it, though this raises nasty lumps (5)
3 Leaves off as a result of this (9)
4 A bit of seed enables one to make a garden (4)
5 The main indication of fluctuation (4-4)
6 Get enthusiastic over many a man of music (5)
7 Suspect damp with decay (8)
8 The French understand a person not buying property (6)
14 They're forever scraping the bottom! (8)
16 Make a song about subordinate being cutting (9)
17 Shrub with small flower – ideal form (8)
18 Painfully secretive about foreign money (6)
20 Tackle the man holding a service on a ship (7)
22 Church without many clergy (5)
24 Rated maybe as skilled employment (5)
25 Lovely article in wood (4)

*This puzzle was solved within 30 minutes by 48 per cent of the competitors at the Birmingham regional final of The Times Collins Dictionaries 1988 Crossword Championship.*

# 32

**Across**

1 Whisky left out, we hear, in the rain (6,4)
6 Postman, so to speak? (4)
9 Field in middle distance (4-6)
10 Needled partners about their opponents (4)
12 After a month, landing another job (12)
15 Completed new tower, and so created new record (9)
17. Spanish pen for bull – or cattle, partly (5)
18 This Italian town's given another name when burnt (5)
19 Arm fleet at sea round North Australian port (9)
20 Catechism ministers aren't in church for (8,4)
24 Forced to retreat? Hard cheese! (4)
25 Still lacking subject for debate (10)
26 Opponents of US to have extra missiles initially (4)
27 Urgent appeal occurred, i.e., after disaster (3,2,5)

**Down**

1 Part of London that's so violent? Not East end (4)
2 City's slow first half in scoreless draw (4)
3 State, as usual, is above the law, wrongfully (12)
4 The Italian fellow may be seen around here (5)
5 Forecasting support in action against investment (9)
7 Better order meal before I make speech (10)
8 Acquire wine for some princes (10)
11 Boy with wind instrument almost joined orchestra (12)
13 Following what French agreement's about (10)
14 Restore a green tree after damage (10)
16 It's bad to turn red under the weather (3,6)
21 Place for riding once (5)
22 The dog with the furtive look, people call it (4)
23 The sternest among Russian leaders? (4)

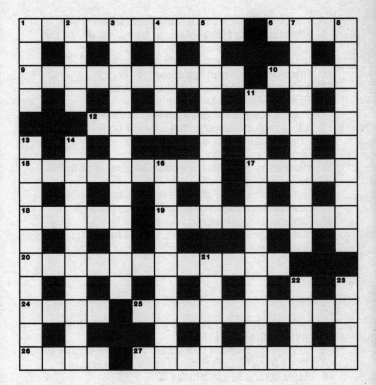

# 33

## Across

1 Monkey's chasing boy, an impudent fellow (10)
6 What the dying Hotspur's time must have (at the end of his sentence?) (4)
10 State hand-out enjoyed by the old clergyman? (7)
11 This Tommy I heard is a detective (7)
12 No hunter caught out with this weapon (9)
13 Flier made lunar landing (5)
14 Change of air? First question for one in Baghdad (5)
15 Is this confection somewhat near the bone? (9)
17 Grim situation here on board (9)
20 Located – by eye, say? (5)
21 Allow entry to technology establishment after notice (5)
23 Thor's hammer the prototype of this missile? (9)
25 Lines of litter scattered round the ring (7)
26 Caber is tossed in an old Italian city (7)
27 In the air he apparently can't fly, this bird (4)
28 Goes in for proverbially profitable commercial activity (10)

## Down

1 Both ends lost after pointed attack put on by highlander at the front (5)
2 Clause not amended in Roman magistrate's office (9)
3 How a friend signs off nicely at tea perhaps? (14)
4 Player inserts key in a lock (7)
5 Wipe out, quietly, African antelope turning up in the river (7)
7 Insect soaring about with sharp ringing sound (5)
8 Introduced one now in charge of publication (9)
9 It is held up by sundry eastern men in the way of musical entertainment (14)
14 On the spot when ten trains crashed (9)
16 How a great 4 affects us when making one of these (9)
18 Went round with it in a gold couch (7)
19 Distress at losing a hundred kopecks (7)

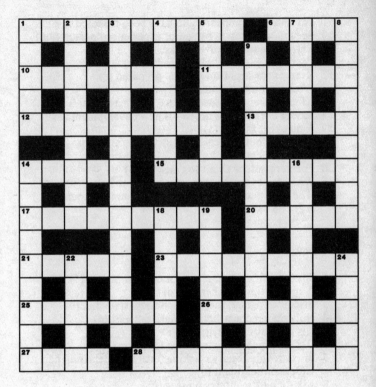

22 Hampton Court feature includes one serial, we hear (5)
24 Pot concealing a snake? (5)

# 34

**Across**

1 Far away, not appearing to have been troubled (6-6)
9 Speculator taken in by senior experienced person (3,6)
10 Retreating waters reveal vessel (5)
11 Pacific empire Nicholas absorbed (6)
12 Kind of construction manual prepared (8)
13 Whittington as painter? (6)
15 Kind of licence needed for ace pilot's aerobatics (8)
18 Easing of tension is noted – a new development (8)
19 A race tip? Listen! (6)
21 Breaking foot, totters a bit (8)
23 Appointment with a girl (6)
26 Former student about to crack up (5)
27 What drives Greek character back into battle (9)
28 Rise about noon in river is beyond human experience (12)

**Down**

1 Silver on first appearance for old competitor (7)
2 Plant needing Southern border (5)
3 Biscuit designed, they say, to follow state diet (9)
4 Holy men reconstructing image out east (4)
5 His relations may tell tales (8)
6 Old money in notes smoothed the way (5)
7 Brave revolutionary tracking territorial detachment under commandant (8)
8 Ask for a little money on ring (6)
14 Revised plans for radical water transport (8)
16 Advocates getting in money to build large food store (5,4)
17 Ararat perhaps for man out in storm (8)
18 Bear – with a sore head possibly? (6)
20 Police search operation is granted broadcast (4-3)
22 A second's start would give obvious pleasure to this runner (5)
24 Triumph obvious in Lawrence yarn (5)
25 Books in charge of auditors (4)

# 35

## Across

1 One may be pushed to cope with natural growth (4-5)
6 Solids initially efficacious when eaten by young creatures (5)
9 Greek character on horseback confronting wild lions (7)
10 Singer of lines about the French, written when hostilities end? (7)
11 Breathe one's last during a University valediction (5)
12 Third man of little significance – but what publicity! (9)
14 Wood found in a tray? (3)
15 Cell diagram incorporating circle – it's in code (11)
17 A singular complaint from a prophet of Judah (11)
19 Ermine, would you say? (3)
20 Archdeacon with fantastic zeal seen around posh eastern state (9)
22 Not in a whisper – permitted to be heard (5)
24 Man devoured by a tiger, say – a circus employee (7)
26 Like Rossini and his girl in Algiers (7)
27 Run in the next race (5)
28 Joke in a kindly way, or with sarcasm? (9)

## Down

1 She left before dawn, having no alternative (5)
2 Petulant, or used to be? Nonsense! (7)
3 Over the States and Canada, gangster's female accomplice is clam-like (9)
4 Newly leased building for sheep (11)
5 Bank dispute (3)
6 Piece of jewellery for a girl student (5)
7 26 city register found in Oban, perhaps (7)
8 Litter found in the rack, for example (9)
13 Going over to decimals – can one term it love for reform? (11)
14 Lessen evil, possibly, in a recent case (9)
16 Geneva site includes a gaudy pub (3-6)
18 Bird turned up three times in the turret (7)
19 Purchases may deplete his stocks (7)

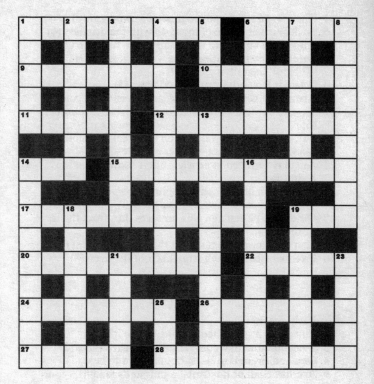

21 This animal is crossed in the interests of survival (5)
23 Fine openers from Dyfed (5)
25 The end of the dump! (3)

## 36

**Across**

1 The way to stimulate progress of a swimmer (8)
5 Nick Weaver is one of those up with the drinkers (6)
10 Air supply needed to make this organ function (5)
11 Oriental isle gets into a mess with this issue (9)
12 'Turnip!' the rallying cry? (9)
13 Whence Roland, bearing good news (5)
14 Armour of copper is clothing an Abyssinian prince (7)
16 Here to witness an international sporting encounter (6)
19 Put, say, Maltese award up on the breakfast table (3-3)
21 Look over the circuit-breaker muddle (7)
23 Awful rot written in articles, but it comes from the heart (5)
25 Put back in office, control political community (9)
27 This time-keeper's wasted, we hear (9)
28 Quick as a pedestrian who emerges thus from the traffic (5)
29 Learned cleric enters race at this half-way point (6)
30 Picture biscuits taken straight from the oven (8)

**Down**

1 Early snack? (8)
2 Pint guest mishandled – doing this to it? (9)
3 Drag up honoured companion from the ravine (5)
4 One endless old drinking-bout is hard to bear (7)
6 Ape has most of the fruit – a nut perhaps (5-4)
7 Having the stomach for an excursion east (5)
8 Very little time (6)
9 She joins George the writer and artist (6)
15 Raphael, the affable one – it might be the port (9)
17 Easily nauseated by poor production of his masque (9)
18 For ever enthralled apparently, showing devout respect (8)
20 Father locks up a social outcast (6)
21 'Now sleeps the _____ petal, now the white' (Tennyson) (7)
22 One of two measures called by Mark Twain (6)

*This puzzle was solved within 30 minutes by 57 per cent of the competitors at the 1988 Glasgow regional final of The Times Collins Dictionaries Crossword Championship.*

24 Ring the canon (5)
26 Supernaturally acute (5)

# 37

**Across**

1 Fruitful result completed by second-hand addition (6)
5 Distinguished or undistinguished person (8)
9 Crew under control in vehicle (4-2-4)
10 Originator of intrigue in the past (4)
11 Cunning part of bridgehead (8)
12 Ignore reforms in the country's administrative division (6)
13 Duck and swan up in the air (4)
15 Bananas he will put in fruit container (8)
18 Is blues composed without a single composer? (8)
19 Painful choice at the crossroads, perhaps (4)
21 Dried fruit is getting wet, apparently (6)
23 Reasonable desert island with lake (8)
25 Judge's conclusions in hard case are firm (4)
26 One who analysed orbits in form of pure conics (10)
27 Royal person in cape surrounded by newsmen (8)
28 The last one across! (6)

**Down**

2 Foreign capital upset about university affair (5)
3 Rod and cane, possibly? Possibly (9)
4 Partners on river stray off course (6)
5 Standard indications of military rank (5,3,7)
6 Mild temper (8)
7 Begin with heart transplant for this creature (5)
8 Follow appropriate sign of clerical occupation (3-6)
14 Soldier king joined armed vessel (9)
16 Though Wells wrote some, his essays include none (9)
17 Top Liberal in tender embrace (8)
20 Bones discovered, in consternation (6)
22 Simpleton lacking penny, a hindrance for him (5)
24 Blue first then last in series on river (5)

## 38

**Across**

1 On the continent, I experienced war (5)
4 Chastise wanton whores with it (9)
9 Hurry up and move forward (4,5)
10 Festival's prize sent back (5)
11 Ms Greenaway involves gunmen in fighting (6)
12 Fish and insects turn a drab colour (5-3)
14 What you would call us in explosive contest (10)
16 Try to sell a bird (4)
19 Prophet deprived of a pipe (4)
20 One who provides a luncheon voucher (4-6)
22 Movingly depict an academic (8)
23 Kidnap and return Brown's child (6)
26 Prone to deception (5)
27 Instruct unmarried people to lose weight (9)
28 Same party can provide the one who holds the purse strings (9)
29 Watch, for instance, when terms of reference are rejected (5)

**Down**

1 Sailor on boat – he used to work with ropes (4,5)
2 Poet in the right (5)
3 Transferring 500 servicemen can put end to training (8)
4 Gangster pursued by a sheriff (4)
5 Riotous gathering, about 50, represents a quarter of the revolution (5,5)
6 Foreign money subscribed to Royal Commission (6)
7 Pack horse used around States (9)
8 Flourishing ancient city, abandoned by ancient god (5)
13 I'm in prison without money, that's the snag (10)
15 Aid US pays out – it provides reassurance (3-1-5)
17 Horatio Herbert Christopher – a name to shout about (9)
18 A clue, in the main, for time (8)
21 On reflection, a sap holds the key to the puzzle (6)
22 College beginning to prepare for growth (5)

24  It's worshipped in Shinto temples (5)
25  Disparage the rise of Australian football, displacing
    English (4)

**Across**

1 Exercise with a woman and cause some irritation (5)
4 Tax Peter I arranged to abolish (9)
9 Lands fruit – and that's where the main danger is (9)
10 Stop up for the finish (5)
11 Damage in a docking facility (6)
12 Players long past their best wrapped up well (8)
14 A monster bird followed by a second (10)
16 Charitable group (4)
19 Three pupils taking in nothing lounge about (4)
20 Intrudes awkwardly in sea-going craft – or might (10)
22 Sort of banana has insect visible on the outside (8)
23 An oriental cult – therefore without taste (6)
26 Capital atmosphere found in the small business house (5)
27 To do without preparation is better all round (9)
28 Dull-coloured plant on public land (4-5)
29 Within 24 hours the minister will be a father (5)

**Down**

1 One came out badly in the ballot, being controversial (9)
2 Composer of 'The Spanish Fish' (5)
3 A European schoolboy clutching a shilling (8)
4 It's sound, on reflection (4)
5 They never take steps to maintain silence! (3-7)
6 Soldiers give up and fall back (6)
7 Juxtaposed in a scalene triangle (9)
8 Some of the men don't improve (5)
13 Tried if car smash results in manslaughter (10)
15 Grabbing everyone brought up in disheartening sur-roundings (9)
17 Find a record concerning Yorkist leader (9)
18 The flyover? (4,4)
21 High-powered firm (6)
22 Covenants to do something in addition to writing (5)
24 Diana was the making of this nymph (5)
25 Take a turn serving up drinks (4)

# 40

**Across**

1 On motorway, certain about coming accident (12)
9 Teach 150 in special sort of college (9)
10 Give up in pro game (5)
11 City's side at sea in scoreless draw (6)
12 Sounds like obscure Scots explorer in London area (4,4)
13 Cut lumber (6)
15 Her pronouncement's relevant (8)
18 Something soothing spoken in castle (8)
19 Do some stock-taking with odd result (6)
21 Perfectly fit model of pacifism to follow (8)
23 Main force in Troy, for example (6)
26 Girl waits for its performance (5)
27 Waste one on flight (9)
28 First illustration shows face of building (12)

**Down**

1 Spirits of a sort holding up party procedures (7)
2 Painting becomes firm after a short time (5)
3 Give two pounds, nothing more, to sculptor (9)
4 Terrible ache in a head (4)
5 Scorers mentally switching parts (8)
6 Sounds like coarse fish (5)
7 Player given an awful roasting (8)
8 Inexperienced soldier that is attached to castle (6)
14 Release, in a manner of speaking (8)
16 Cheese that's demonstrated success in long run (9)
17 A couple of boys in Essex town (8)
18 Clothing articles dropped by Boadicea (6)
20 Understanding contents of ten, in triplicate (7)
22 Rebel who became US president (5)
24 For audience, could be chaps making appearance (5)
25 Endlessly on the go in Italian town (4)

# 41

## Across

1 After onset of sickness, make slow progress – sound right poorly (6)
5 Take a second Shakespearian heroine (8)
9 Youth devouring Greek character; and vice versa (8)
10 Army to wear natty field dressing (6)
11 Explorer is eating last of the sledge dogs (8)
12 It's poetic to chase the sea nymph (6)
13 Plane tree middling wet after drizzle (8)
15 Formerly in the City: no return (4)
17 Forest administrator (4)
19 So successful I left Masefield floundering (4-4)
20 Wall to keep Bill away from home? (6)
21 Orbital extreme observed from a sort of pinhole (8)
22 Arrange to publish Russian decree (6)
23 A show of spirit is difficult to forget (8)
24 Book an hour in the Plough (8)
25 What the parrot did had repercussions (6)

## Down

2 Toast for a fat man? (4-4)
3 Write off for a slot (8)
4 I'm a fan of the don, so I take exam in vacation (9)
5 Eat fish crumbled with bread, for they combine well (5,2,1,7)
6 Bird in the hand, or foot (7)
7 At first it's natural to catch cold just sitting about (8)
8 He is one with an early epistle (8)
14 Way home from the pub (9)
15 Display of temper abroad over plumbing emergency (8)
16 Solid block of cars (8)
17 How to pedal to coast (8)
18 Tell everyone girl is overweight (8)
19 Clients' letters bashed out – from this? (7)

# 42

## Across

1 Account holder has son to maintain (5)
4 Dark horse at twenty to one possibly causing an upset (9)
9 No action required about coach reservation (9)
10 Standard exercise included in examination (5)
11 With the head away, afraid to give a severe reprimand (6)
12 A case is essential back in Lincoln (8)
14 Crash start by new driver on other side of junction (6-4)
16 Runner unfit after finish of canter (4)
19 Was sorry for being rough, say (4)
20 One of the team in the long grass is called back (10)
22 Selkirk perhaps found here? No, elsewhere (8)
23 Source material used for study programme (6)
26 Submit a return (5)
27 I am to introduce summary note? That's not quite accurate (9)
28 Pronouncement from Church after extreme article (9)
29 Put up before court (5)

## Down

1 Way to set up motorists' travel agency in USA (9)
2 It is abandoned by caller for face-saving purposes (5)
3 Revised itinerary – engineers arranging detour (8)
4 Upright fellow (4)
5 Dismissive instruction to firefighters? (2,2,6)
6 Pickwickian put up on island (6)
7 Cause of current build-up if one is put in wide river (9)
8 Always poetical – that's strange (5)
13 Change into a later fashion (10)
15 Parcel post never made a loss (9)
17 Freemasons, perhaps, on square footing (9)
18 Former pupil, the only one Lawrence dated (8)
21 Fat monarch found in food store (6)
22 Turned up in support of shy creature (5)

24  Rear gunner is superior to enemy initially (5)
25  Weapon mounted in deep emplacement (4)

# 43

**Across**

1 Refuse to mock (5)
4 Property man employed by picture's producer (9)
9 Dish for a penny, or something very similar (9)
10 Succeeded as student, say, with a course of Italian (5)
11 Recollect meeting (5)
12 Lamenting reform in dressing (9)
13 Key property to develop in one's mind (7)
15 Diabolical measure is hard on both sides (7)
18 Yonder stands a saint (7)
20 In 23, in short, always different (7)
21 Company, after month, game for Merchant of Venice (5,4)
23 Jocular retort as reaction to investment (5)
25 Genius adds point to political protest (5)
26 Awkward situation inflamed King Edward, perhaps (3,6)
27 Person given something as attender of meeting (9)
28 Craft shown by putting Arthurian knight in front of a king (5)

**Down**

1 Follow Tories, getting control over work (9)
2 Leader of female trio appearing annually (5)
3 Beginning in fantasy, a distortion of reality (5-4)
4 Bloomer possibly fatal for boxer (7)
5 Disappear with end of emperor in Japan, perhaps (7)
6 Nobody's child called after this flower? (5)
7 Behind Bill, going around South American city (9)
8 Food of a sort that's been cooked (5)
14 He produces changes in steamer's direction (9)
16 Farm animals exist to breed (9)
17 Joint support for tree and another plant (9)
19 A second eleven's unidentified player (7)
20 Dog that is following author from same country (7)
21 Wine warmed occasionally? Some of it is (5)
22 Previously you reportedly trapped this wild animal (5)
24 Lake disaster with yacht's bow letting in water (5)

# 44

**Across**

1 Whitebait for those selective dieters? (6)
5 Guernsey from The Needles, say (8)
9 Done with farm butter, I produce seasoned beef (8)
10 Dance-the-light-fantastic time (6)
11 Ruler-angle indicates Mulloway (4-4)
12 Stock-controller's pen (6)
13 In the longer parts, A1 may be characteristic of the North perhaps (8)
15 Greek inventor who took lead (4)
17 Firm way to estimate price (4)
19 This canine is a biter on sight (3-5)
20 Well! Ten French flowers in a spike (6)
21 Formerly a prospector whom Pippa satisfied? (8)
22 A waif is into sin (6)
23 Failure of oxygen given to Apollo personnel (8)
24 Jack from the pack, or those dealt to one player? (4-4)
25 Port for modern or ancient craft (6)

**Down**

2 Air Heep's developed as hypocrite in the book (8)
3 Self-banking old flying-machine (8)
4 Economically alone without equality (9)
5 Was he dubbed a highwayman (6,2,3,4)
6 Football official in work is in clover (7)
7 Place of opportunity in Anfield – or a dozen other grounds (8)
8 Strangely solitary cavalier (8)
14 Greatest respect for commercial delivery (9)
15 Where to place the bowler when taken off? (3,5)
16 Passionate movement in music (8)
17 When cutting, it drives round the links (5-3)
18 Opening of indirect access (4-4)
19 Final judgement on a tablet? (7)

# 45

**Across**

1 Indignation shown when last bit of foliage drops out of floral arrangement (5)
4 Royal icing to decorate the base of a macaroon (4-5)
9 Troubled over what's broadcast (5,4)
10 Divided about wearing reversed jacket (5)
11 Being ten per cent, I typify a percentage (6)
12 Bishop back without the rest (8)
14 Improvident compositor may be seedy (3,2,5)
16 It precedes the final passion (4)
19 The bird to change colour, they say (4)
20 Blue shellfish (10)
22 Finally in command of foreign soil, in undisputed command (8)
23 Spinner's pride's hurt (6)
26 At a distance, a look from . . . (5)
27 . . . cold man lacking guile (9)
28 Hand poet mutton chops (9)
29 The address one should use, oddly, for the dead (5)

**Down**

1 Unfinished due to bad weather – drawn (6,3)
2 Assume there'll be trouble with exercises (5)
3 In fifth form, one to get on (3,2,3)
4 Staff hold a course (4)
5 Breaking out of thin cover, a deer (10)
6 The way you attach an Afghan (6)
7 Counterfeit coin has to move slowly – flow limited by banks (9)
8 Run after stock car used in competition (5)
13 Seductive summons (4-6)
15 Held short assembly as a starting point (9)
17 Dissertations about gold – one speculates (9)
18 Expedition made by 29 to beauty spot (8)
21 Leaders of Comanches, Ojibwas and Navahos have super pow-wow (6)
22 Pulls the grass up (5)

*This puzzle was solved within 30 minutes by 17 per cent of the competitors at the 1988 Leeds regional final of The Times Collins Dictionaries Crossword Championship.*

24 Pop round about alarm (5)
25 Die from sword-thrust (4)

# 46

**Across**

1 What was left of woman's sex appeal years after (8)
5 Mars I'd gather would never do it (6)
9 Whereby a beast is led by the nose to its place of slaughter (8)
10 State vote against the bottle (6)
12 Refuge for deserters (5)
13 Perfume, free to wearers (4-5)
14 Not the proper sphere for Gilbert's sharp (8,4)
18 Where to keep secret place for private amusement (2,4,6)
21 Singular devout mass sung by Negroes (9)
23 Call for trick, holding nothing (5)
24 Crossing point for planes beginning here (6)
25 Somehow I tug in five, but he gets away (8)
26 Attempt to include conclusion with it (6)
27 Christmas present drawer (8)

**Down**

1 Something's cooking, but his choice is take it or leave it (6)
2 Appreciate the flavour (6)
3 The visitors' counter (9)
4 Simple denial army commander has to give out (7,5)
6 Relatively opposed to Robin Hood, say (2-3)
7 Where time-servers entered by the Golden Gate (8)
8 Ape ordinary soldier on military exercise (8)
11 Let out provision of the Penal Code? (6,6)
15 Amusing way around (9)
16 Bob identifies two causes of power failure (3,5)
17 Definite sign of an increase (8)
19 Flat out putting up American deal (6)
20 Remote disintegrating body from outer space (6)
22 Heroic tale of an Irish house I erected (5)

# 47

1 David and Sam split difference (8)
5 Condiment cut by skipper (6)
8 By river, a number cultivate a plant (10)
9 Central European pearl collection (4)
10 Investor in music business watching all one's acts? (9,5)
11 Replace fruit out of tin with a vegetable (7)
13 Clean habits perhaps getting Californian city down (7)
15 Lexicographer's tea-makers (7)
18 One's embracing bowler, perhaps, as bosom pal (7)
21 Receivers admit pearls, etc., mostly reset, need fake guarantees (5,9)
22 Take hat round beach near Venice (4)
23 Instrument the orchestra leader toiled to adjust (10)
24 Devious move before close of play (6)
25 Put money back into check garment (8)

## Down

1 Mix up spray for aquatic plant (7)
2 Grotesque contour in rock formation (9)
3 It's not important about island (7)
4 Smart and fashionable inside? Contemptible (7)
5 Vehicle for Semite in accident, almost (9)
6 Pattern from quiet part of Spain (7)
7 Rebuff concerning seeds (7)
12 Find fault with something in log, working with wood (9)
14 For example, French force's member (9)
16 Service on course is vulgar (7)
17 Rich source no longer available (4,3)
18 A partnership not everyone found dreadful (7)
19 Weeding stopped, apparently, for this dance (3-4)
20 Upsets constituents about Conservative? It's doubtful (7)

# 48

**Across**

1  Secret of breaking out without injury (4-4)
6  Crushed wood – it is used to make a desk (6)
9  Chaffer gets horse in draw (6)
10  An apology for a dance (6-2)
11  Board with a bird, one who's slovenly (8)
12  Young devils encircle the Spanish forces (6)
13  Measures ladder (5)
14  Possibly a man-eater, a girl a lot involved (9)
17  Required by law to be almost a model politician (9)
19  20 moving out of range (5)
22  What Cockney wife-beater does, we hear – this'll cure him (6)
23  Before being worn, a garment is returned, showing slight damage (8)
24  Home of the retiring bluefish (8)
25  In bed I will turn pale (6)
26  Artist given food, a bit of salad (6)
27  Always over there, English people (8)


**Down**

2  Fellow rented a wreath (7)
3  In a difficult situation, use hose on grass. . . (5,4)
4  . . . found in this jacket (6)
5  Three people, in general, treat learner badly (7,8)
6  With cards, I can stop (4,2,2)
7  Here's a donation (7)
8  Prize given to the right officer (9)
13  Something worn by Jack Ketch? (9)
15  Shy member of the family (4,5)
16  Marine creature has first to undergo a metamorphosis (8)
18  Flavouring also I perceive in it (7)
20  Rising best-seller is a sensation (7)
21  Like 5, left among the rubbish (6)

# 49

**Across**

1 Bows? Not likely! (12)
9 A nuisance having to follow one pursuing a false trail (9)
10 Graduates thus as a singer (5)
11 Deserving a reprimand (6)
12 The case of the blackleg poet (8)
13 Standards for the French backing a horse (6)
15 Reform one Tory act – it's an outrage (8)
18 Discourage introduction of tin container for wine (8)
19 Looked intently for members of the second and fourth estates (6)
21 Concerning some filming in pass (8)
23 Don't hurry – that's the way with bread (6)
26 Samuel's teacher turns to George (5)
27 Which place is said to entertain approval? (9)
28 The turbulent masses resent change of 11 (12)

**Down**

1 Loud rough leader of the Northern States (7)
2 Plan to have a drink, say (5)
3 This knight may see a female smile (9)
4 Kind of music that has spirit (4)
5 Show for many in Bharat, note (8)
6 Food like baby's beef extract (5)
7 Framework for pearls? That's odd (8)
8 Time for Gilbert's classical pops (6)
14 Russian police chief's about turn which may cause ill-feeling (8)
16 Upsets patent tea-makers (9)
17 Daredevil told not to do so much damage (8)
18 He owes more than the cattle-dealer (6)
20 The joy of the Camptown ladies (7)
22 Championship of the right (5)
24 Colour of wood (5)
25 The devil's mischief for these hands (4)

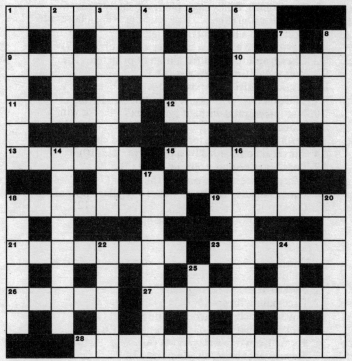

*This puzzle was solved within 30 minutes by 32 per cent of the competitors in the 1988 Leeds regional final of The Times Collins Dictionaries Crossword Championship.*

# 50

**Across**

1 The French, following a plan, get shady trees (6)
4 Flag, as usual (8)
10 Conducted a bag search (7)
11 Revive with a little relaxation and a mineral (7)
12 Cheers amid reform for a man of principle (10)
13 Well-established business (4)
15 Country music composer (7)
17 The outcome of pressure here will be a letting off (7)
19 Not interrupted without purpose (7)
21 A neat drive (5-2)
23 With due deference for both state and church (4)
24 Travel accompanied by a fellow worker (10)
27 Possibly it's not a stopping-place (7)
28 Where to see a large bird by the water (7)
29 Late in the day the head makes a regular appearance (8)
30 Coming nowadays before the opening (6)

**Down**

1 Spread at sea to entrap fish (9)
2 Face pain with spirit (7)
3 Given aid, created trouble and got out (10)
5 Hill guide who causes much anguish (9)
6 Home from one's travels (4)
7 Loving phone-call after a party (7)
8 Mother set about some soldiers – fancy! (5)
9 New keys made for the island (4)
14 Timekeeper is little help (6-4)
16 Doesn't take into consideration special reductions (9)
18 Having to do with jailed social worker being ashamed (9)
20 Shorten the time taken to provide port facilities (7)
22 Estate many men see split up (7)
23 Over a quarter may be of imitation stone (5)
25 Stood up for a woman (4)
26 The attitude of people receiving one (4)

# 51

**Across**

1 Sounds like this, we hear? Just the reverse (9)
6 Criminal procrastination, for example (5)
9 Is equivalent of stops at sea (5,2)
10 Furniture – late rather than early Adam (7)
11 It can be used to dig up allotment. . . (5)
12 . . . and scatter hay round unusual garden shrub (9)
14 Rubbish removed from 4 (3)
15 Ornate piece of work for mending cardinal's robe (6,5)
17 Prayer that can be uplifting for people (11)
19 Impair – cut out odd bits? (3)
20 Reduce volumes in balance (9)
22 Roused the eccentric out of bed (3,2)
24 Very large problem to capture river animal (7)
26 Writer in fighting form turns to large book (7)
27 Navy getting positive vote before long (5)
28 Purify with scent if I'd made a mess (9)

**Down**

1 Race in sea 'aze, so to speak (5)
2 Tough six-footer gets many parts in pictures (4-3)
3 Complaint could make Pluto rage (9)
4 British poet remaining inside association (11)
5 Aim for goal in close finish (3)
6 It's the eighth letter of alphabet, note (5)
7 Understanding in mind proverbially must be so (7)
8 Flock in direction of fold (9)
13 Harmful enough to destroy us going about the city (11)
14 Company store (9)
16 Temple concerned with exalting some female (9)
18 Boy put up a high shot in game where win follows draw (7)
19 Marathon leader on flat surface changing often (7)
21 Writer with nibs and pen starts off (5)
23 Assume one is employed? (5)
25 It's not clear what black sheep's name is (3)

# 52

**Across**

1 Meiosis in T. S. Eliot play (7)
5 E.g. Rosemary and Theo involved in Rossetti's group (7)
9 Cause of lumps in a jersey? (6-3)
10 Splendid organ-effect (5)
11 Die to make an impression (5)
12 Art of constructing moving rock Masses, say (9)
14 Composition of rocks for some pretty rich model (14)
17 The nerve of Thomas Percy – such bottle! (9,5)
21 His policy is to go in for huge excesses (9)
23 Love area of bracing air (5)
24 Reverse reel features curved figures (5)
25 Wild dream that produced a progressive party-leader (3,6)
26 Game in which one can lose one's marbles, being knocked out (4-3)
27 The place for vehicles when theatreland has black-out (7)

**Down**

1 Most reasonable to behold direction of bright land (6)
2 Land given to church for row of houses (7)
3 But it is not related to the Dutch elm (5-4)
4 Shooting-brake? (6-5)
5 Make regular journeys in the Strand (3)
6 Some of his *Aminta*'s so pastoral (5)
7 English law expert and poet (7)
8 Sikes's pet sweetmeat (5-3)
13 Girl perhaps exciting crowd with pair of hips for a start (5-6)
15 Lady Smitton, we hear, in Italy (9)
16 Last of 'Pussycat' represents Edward L. as nonsense-writer (8)
18 This towelling is friction-reduced (3,4)
19 Amerind Watch Co gone bust (7)
20 Enthusiastic rating (6)

22 Riding-school accident (5)
25 More, say, for one of the greedy guts (3)

**Across**

1 Figure of a child has moved me to show up (3,2,5)
6 Bath the setting for this opera? (4)
10 Characteristic noise heard from car that's exchanged (5-2)
11 Some hundred Germans aboard this boat (7)
12 Not straight – future too unsettled (3,2,4)
13 Get out of bed about noon and wash (5)
14 Transport firm has a lot of pain (5)
15 Execute Duke – His Grace has misbehaved (9)
17 Appropriate animals to see how the land lies (4,5)
20 You can carve with this provided the joint's almost round (5)
21 Called me in and relaxed (5)
23 Profit from backing book about light (9)
25 Broadcast from Russia about retrogressive university (7)
26 Difficult week in a hospital room (7)
27 By the sound of it, is familiar with the organ (4)
28 Reds salute uncommonly scarlet woman (10)

**Down**

1 Shoot at kinkajou (5)
2 Someone admired joint of meat found on the breakfast table (5-4)
3 Before long shoes do any feet wrong (3,2,5,4)
4 Old part of the country without an underhand organisation (7)
5 Finish up in service – such folly! (7)
7 Barrel, perhaps, not originally for mounting a horse (5)
8 In school, at all times keep going (9)
9 Ring is blue (4,3,7)
14 Clear out of copper – bronze demand about right (3,3,3)
16 Say again and again bond is up in value (9)
18 Upset queen, embracing priest, went too far (7)
19 Smarty-boots was nearly dumped in a barrow (4-3)

22 Chap needing a great deal (5)
24 Movements at sea – i.e., when the bottom surfaces (5)

# 54

**Across**

1 Vessel is a mile in length (6)
4 One in a position to make a come-back? (8)
10 Wine from Port of Spain? (9)
11 A pound short in the balance (5)
12 Sort of chips you get in such an industrial valley (7)
13 Notice record prize draw that is not wanted (7)
14 Matron perhaps getting medicine right (5)
15 Light car for railwaymen? (8)
18 Galleries between Dover and Ashford (8)
20 Cattle hard to find in Wales (5)
23 Wooster gives suit to Jeeves (7)
25 She was entitled to succeed in the play (7)
26 Nonsensical fellow with a name to memorise (5)
27 Generally at home with shorthand (2,7)
28 Training horses in period costume? No, just the opposite (8)
29 Settler holding royal petition (6)

**Down**

1 Squash – several games per team (3,5)
2 Game of wits (7)
3 The five-hundred-pound enigma – a prickly one? (9)
5 An educational facility for the Penzance band? (8-6)
6 Island lives under historical measure (5)
7 Board to a university in dramatic scene (7)
8 Discussion would be needed first for this girl to become housekeeper (6)
9 Rural revels – turkey-trotting, for example (7,7)
16 One of several supporters in rail hold-up (9)
17 Huntsman has damage to curse about (8)
19 Zealously copy one with feathers behind (7)
21 Useful service from the little woman, about a point up (7)
22 Climbed, then peeled off (6)
24 Sign in front of take-away (5)

*This puzzle was solved within 30 minutes by 17 per cent of the competitors in the 1988 Glasgow regional final of The Times Collins Dictionaries Crossword Championship.*

# 55

**Across**

1 American misses Lake District (6)
5 Appear depressed in final confrontation (4-4)
9 Completed twice? That's excessive (8)
10 Measure inch, initially, as part of foot (6)
11 Student's ill-gotten gain (8)
12 Hockey teams in group unfair to women, usually (6)
13 Butter gives a smoother finish to pastry (8)
15 Unruly youngster is ring-leader in strike (4)
17 Lighter transport for small person (4)
19 City of David, figuratively speaking (8)
20 Bridge expert in court (6)
21 Piano piece – a very small one (8)
22 Painter shows archbishop in his church (6)
23 Thugs mounted attacks in violent way (6,2)
24 Legal clerks collecting senorita's letters (8)
25 Land's End or place in another county (6)

**Down**

2 Critic about to join one of the audience (8)
3 Crate containing vent put on ship (8)
4 Deficiency neither Alice nor Humpty Dumpty had (9)
5 Magazine ostentatiously displays crowd-pullers (9,6)
6 Cheerless – wet and rainy without a break (7)
7 Scout dismissed special condition (8)
8 Poem isn't rewritten – Pope's fault (8)
14 Act like milkman? Philander (3,6)
15 Tower of London's complex (8)
16 Human production – painting, poem, part of play (8)
17 Annoying type is a casualty (8)
18 Hand record over in an interval (8)
19 Cover, for example, most of one tree with another (7)

# 56

**Across**

1 Check Murphy is coming back (5)
4 Book cover has to repeat the title (9)
9 Abandoned grotto crumbling into the marsh (9)
10 Get state permit to have a servant (5)
11 Huge cost of electrical safety precaution (5)
12 So sure to make a discovery (9)
13 Ate basin of sea food (7)
15 Big cars on the US Atlantic seaboard? (7)
18 Go back to buy another round (7)
20 Inconvenienced by action to suppress poem (7)
21 Lack of energy deters sin that is fashionable (9)
23 King to weaken, until Parsifal wins this? (5)
25 Put one in store – a wee one (5)
26 One way to be delivered from the emperor (9)
27 Take spare writing implement, in a way, out of pocket (9)
28 Where one would find a wandering shade? (5)

**Down**

1 Kind of course fee (9)
2 Less draped about in silks (5)
3 Tempting, but it can bite a few people (9)
4 High passage makes jazz freak move his feet (7)
5 Criticise a guerrilla's swagger (7)
6 Sound examples of it are D and X, both ending in C (5)
7 Everyone in support of high-level operation shows courage (9)
8 Bird perched on an enormous man (5)
14 Decide to set boy up with the trappings of rank (9)
16 Get great help working the scoreboard (9)
17 Secondary activities include minor verse (9)
19 Blandishments well described by Dormouse (7)
20 Due to eat second course (7)
21 It's forbidden to put a native inside (5)
22 Repudiate saint – he's French (5)
24 Advanced to a crisis (5)

56

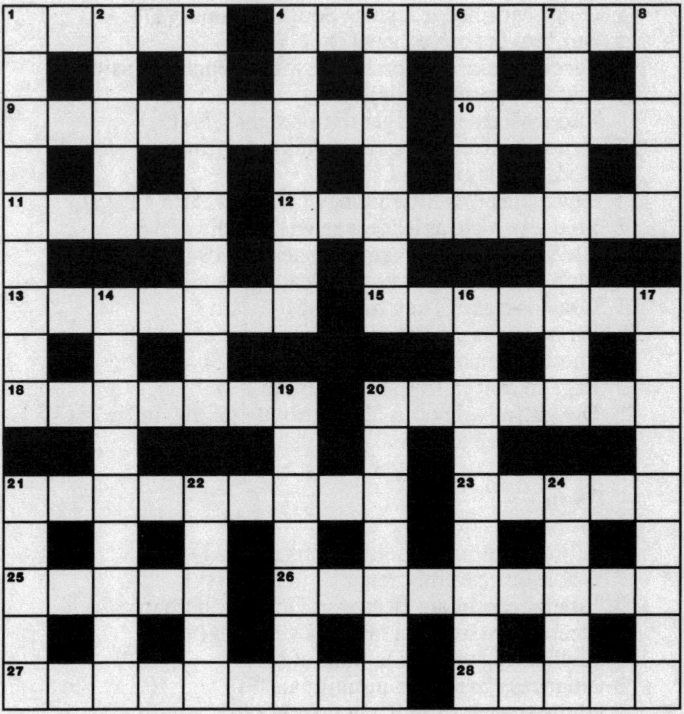

# 57

**Across**

1 Court card needed, since South is dummy (7)
5 Burdens for mules, say (7)
9 Forcibly take over on horse, with French on inside (5)
10 Lighter propeller (5-4)
11 End a Metro trip to get to this sight? (5,4)
12 Venue for Council once dividing Nottingham (5)
13 Vocal guides in the City (5)
15 Consisting of a little money I have as extra pay (9)
18 Mad and vicious leaders reign so badly (9)
19 Old picture I found among back copies (5)
21 Map out *Daily Telegraph*'s leader (5)
23 Coast is clear? Then turn (4-5)
25 Wren, for example, reveals her tactic at sea (9)
26 Poet's gloomy daughter to bring up (5)
27 Page to rent in free sheet, perhaps (7)
28 Delightfully devious about minute taking, initially (7)

**Down**

1 Adjourn although holding this record (7)
2 Noble female embracing 50 in legion (9)
3 Liberal candidate elected in October, perhaps (5)
4 Deep down, recollect Burma's in East (9)
5 Enchanting woman left out of set (5)
6 Nuances obvious to individuals (9)
7 Made speech supporting member (5)
8 Respect is in order for this (7)
14 Rehearsal? It's a case of political expedience (4,5)
16 Pieces a pound in cost, perhaps (9)
17 Execute, beheading naive people? Exactly! (9)
18 Darling boy, an angel (7)
20 Loathing amount of work associate brings in (7)
22 Seas are hidden by 'aze, we hear, in tropical port (5)
23 Flying boats (5)
24 Jam in a slice of cake (5)

**Across**

1 Fanciful idler – he's well liked (8)
5 Charming things, though they're not long-lasting (6)
10 This will be seen all around the bull ring (5)
11 It's reprehensible to make money over a game (9)
12 For state to pursue private transport would be a bloomer (9)
13 Held by college lecturers due to take up appointments (5)
14 Really stupid, like doubly trendy egghead (7)
16 Provide excitement in extremely smooth, figure-hugging dress (6)
19 A track for climbers (6)
21 Check, and find crawler has pocketed money (7)
23 Traps specially designed for small fish (5)
25 To limit the drink makes good sense (9)
27 'And keep you in the rear of your —' (*Hamlet*) (9)
28 A person who can be relied on should never be dropped (5)
29 Very hard and slippery creature in a foul place (6)
30 The man willing to have a pot at gold (8)

**Down**

1 Mac's a riot – can juggle (8)
2 Birds alight on the fence (9)
3 Breezy point up country here (5)
4 The origin of a waterfall? (3-4)
6 Soft grain, inferior but still highly esteemed (9)
7 Turner's given a trainee two different articles (5)
8 Issue a word of thanks for the music (6)
9 One's after a fellow – a most presentable young man (6)
15 When idle it can break just the same (9)
17 Worker trying to make good takes the blame first (9)
18 Someone not suited for running (8)
20 It's so lethargic – prod it to move (6)
21 Strained to get in double figures – the beginning of the end! (7)

22 Commentaries for Tests? (6)
24 Weapon of the Left in general (5)
26 Go round – otherwise a scrap will result (5)

**Across**

1 Set meal and free bed at hotel (5,5)
6 Sea captain who married a Jezebel (4)
9 Safe blower who started series of small explosions (5,5)
10 Once a capital silver artist (4)
12 Tom's furtive look (4)
13 NCO cut an honour (5-4)
15 Found goose very unyielding (4,4)
16 Sound rugby forward is a smoker (6)
18 Range of colours, say, shows a sense of taste (6)
20 Simple spread – wild duck? (8)
23 Disastrous scheme to drug nun's stew (6-3)
24 Sums – little ones (4)
26 Just open for a drink (4)
27 Two people to an office in Rome (10)
28 Boy in a whirl (4)
29 Service chart marker (10)

**Down**

1 Lift elbow to highest point (4)
2 College accounts cause fights for the auditors (7)
3 It's terribly noisy in the grain division (3-9)
4 Hire mixing machine for the family treasure (8)
5 Miniature enthrals Welsh maid (6)
7 Henry King once got behind a rocky ridge (3-4)
8 Gloomy Uriah admits son is family scoundrel (5,5)
11 Additional racehorses in reserve (6,6)
14 School's first head girl is a hare-brained child (10)
17 H. Finn's contribution to the overdrafts manager (8)
19 A feline poet who repels one (7)
21 The representative of justice tears off among the motorists (7)
22 What is needed is no huge change (6)
25 Oh, it's incredible! (4)

## 60

**Across**

1 Lack of medicine for Nobby, it's said (6)
4 It may preclude an advance, the old boy's story being out of copyright (8)
10 He may be rolling and ruling (9)
11 A charge familiar in the Maldives (5)
12 Constant associated with this unit of brightness (7)
13 Under which one may travel without mechanical power (7)
14 State's second rejection of excellent transport system (5)
15 Having damaged wing, loath to fly in sunlight (5-3)
18 Investor in charge of a plant (8)
20 Model question (5)
23 Note written by prime minister about his specious argument (7)
25 Ambassador most of the capital find unenlightened (7)
26 Posh girl seen around University common (5)
27 Dogged 10 *ac* with evidence of debts? (9)
28 Exaggerate merits of surplus merchandise (8)
29 Stir caused by adman concealing one's name (6)

**Down**

1 Hillmen, seen wandering around the boundary (8)
2 Travelling salesman, a member of the band (7)
3 Found in shop, recently made article from the pottery (9)
5 This used to be the place to change for the Brighton Belle (7-7)
6 Trudge along quietly holding up a passenger vehicle (5)
7 Wild cat interrupting dog's turn on the ice (7)
8 Volunteer student is employed in otorhinolaryngology (6)
9 Stupidly ban tin – material for making bearings (9,5)
16 He takes steps to strike repeatedly (3-6)
17 A young kinsman, the lad under the piano (8)

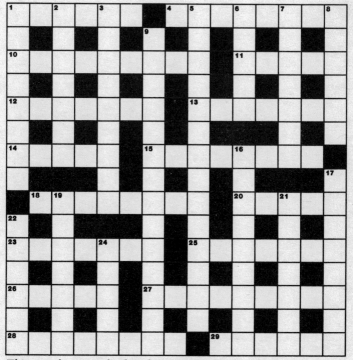

*This puzzle was solved within 30 minutes by 35 per cent of the competitors in the 1988 Birmingham regional final of The Times Collins Dictionaries Crossword Championship.*

19  Compose uplifting melody for last movement of *The Planets* (7)
21  Trains porpoises, perhaps? (7)
22  Does copper represent this in Chilean currency? (6)
24  Fair ones, for example, spoken in passages in church (5)

*Solutions*

# No. 1

| S | C | A | M | P | E | R | | C | U | S | P | A | T | E |
|---|---|---|---|---|---|---|---|---|---|---|---|---|---|---|
| C | | D | | I | | E | | O | | T | | R | | N |
| R | E | M | I | T | | S | O | M | N | O | L | E | N | T |
| U | | I | | C | | I | | B | | N | | A | | R |
| P | O | S | T | H | A | S | T | E | | E | N | S | U | E |
| L | | S | | T | | C | | | | A | | | | A |
| E | D | I | C | T | | A | R | K | W | R | I | G | H | T |
| O | | | | R | | N | | I | | O | | A | | |
| C | O | N | C | E | I | T | E | D | | | P | A | S | T | A |
| A | | A | | | | A | | N | | O | | I | | |
| P | R | E | S | S | | O | R | A | N | G | E | M | E | N |
| I | | X | | U | | T | | P | | R | | E | | T |
| T | U | T | O | R | S | H | I | P | | A | S | T | E | R |
| A | | R | | E | | E | | S | | E | | E | | E |
| L | E | A | N | D | E | R | | R | E | S | E | R | V | E |

# No. 2

| S | C | A | B | B | A | R | D | | N | E | R | E | I | D |
|---|---|---|---|---|---|---|---|---|---|---|---|---|---|---|
| | H | | A | | G | I | A | | | P | | O | | |
| F | A | E | R | I | E | | C | O | U | R | S | I | N | G |
| | M | | T | | O | K | | S | | T | | S | | |
| C | O | L | E | S | L | A | W | | E | X | T | A | N | T |
| | I | | N | | D | H | | A | | P | | O | | |
| A | S | I | D | E | | P | I | S | T | A | C | H | I | O |
| G | | E | | N | | T | | E | | L | | T | | |
| G | E | O | R | G | E | T | T | E | | P | E | A | C | H |
| R | | V | | W | | I | | A | | A | | R | | |
| E | Y | E | F | U | L | | N | E | W | S | R | O | O | M |
| G | | R | | Y | | G | | A | | S | | U | | |
| A | T | T | I | C | W | I | T | | K | N | O | T | T | Y |
| T | | O | | E | | O | | E | | U | | O | | |
| E | S | P | I | E | D | | N | I | N | E | P | I | N | S |

# No. 3

| | F | I | D | D | L | E | S | T | I | C | K | S | |
|---|---|---|---|---|---|---|---|---|---|---|---|---|---|
| B | | O | | E | | A | | T | | R | | E | |
| A | P | R | I | C | O | T | | R | O | O | S | T | E | R |
| C | | S | | L | | T | | I | | N | | C | E | |
| H | O | T | L | I | N | E | | P | E | A | C | H | E | S |
| E | | E | | N | | R | | G | | U | | U | | |
| L | A | R | G | E | | D | I | S | T | E | M | P | E | R |
| O | | | | A | | A | | | | R | | | | |
| R | A | T | E | P | A | Y | E | R | | S | E | R | V | E |
| H | | W | | L | | A | | E | | O | | C | | |
| O | V | E | R | A | C | T | | B | U | M | B | O | A | T |
| O | | L | | T | | I | | A | | I | | K | | I |
| D | E | F | R | O | S | T | | N | A | N | K | E | E | N |
| | T | | O | | H | | D | | A | | R | | G | |
| C | H | A | N | C | E | M | E | D | L | E | Y | |

# No. 4

| T | I | D | E | M | A | R | K | | H | U | M | M | E | L |
|---|---|---|---|---|---|---|---|---|---|---|---|---|---|---|
| O | | I | | E | | U | | Y | | A | | M | | |
| W | A | R | D | E | N | S | H | I | P | | T | U | B | A |
| A | | E | | T | | S | | N | | A | | A | | |
| R | E | C | E | I | V | I | N | G | O | R | D | E | R | |
| D | | T | | N | | F | | | | T | | O | | G |
| S | L | O | U | G | H | Y | | P | I | E | R | R | O | T |
| | R | | E | | | | S | | E | | | | |
| P | A | Y | L | O | A | D | | B | E | L | T | A | N | E |
| | I | | A | | T | | R | | I | | R | | N | |
| R | U | N | T | H | E | G | A | U | N | T | L | E | T | |
| P | | O | | E | | S | | E | | I | | H | | |
| C | O | W | L | | N | E | W | S | M | O | N | G | E | R |
| R | | I | | R | | I | | U | | H | | A | | |
| S | T | I | N | G | Y | | T | E | E | T | O | T | A | L |

**2,** 9 *a.*: Anag. FIRE around A.E. (G.W. Russell, Irish poet).

**3,** 8 *a.*: APR(il) 1(st);   20 *d.*: Alsatia, Whitefriars district of London, a sanctuary for criminals.

**4,** 8 *a.*: Rev. Septimus Harding, Trollope's *The Warden*;   6 *d.*: Veronica – a pass in bull-fighting;   17 *d.*: Lincoln – breed of sheep.

## No. 5

```
C A S T O F F   W O R S T E D
O   I   L   A   I   O   S   E
U N D I D   C O N S O N A N T
R   E   T   E   C   S   R   E
T O C S I N   W H I T T I E R
S   A   M   N   E   N
H O R S E   O B S E R V A N T
I   R   N   T   E       A
P E R I S C O P E   S T I C K
O   N   R   H   N   E
C O U N T E S S   R U S S I A
A   T   R   E   P   F   T   P
B R I T A N N I A   F L O R A
O   N   C   S   L   L   R   R
T H E A T R E   M A E W E S T
```

## No. 6

```
F R A N C I S C A N     S   P
E   O   N   O   E U R O P A
E V E N T F U L   E   N   T
E   U   O   E N D A N G E R
A   S   R   T       B   O
F L E A   M A I D M A R I A N
O   G   A   T   A   R   Y
R E D E A L T   T S A R D O M
E   E   L   I   T   I   I
C O N V E Y A N C E   C H I C
A   O   S   R   K   S
S Q U A R E U P   M   S   R
T   N   A   I R I S H M A N
L O C K E R   R   N   A   E
E   E   N E E R D O W E L L
```

## No. 7

```
F O R T R E S S   A T O M I C
P   A   A   O   S   A   O
R U N N E R   U P S T R E A M
L   G   W   T   A   S   P
F E V E R I S H   S E T T L E
N   R   G   S   S   R   T
S T A I D   R E D I N G O T E
I   N   S   A   N   R   N
D A R E D E V I L   D E B U T
E   A   M   S   A   Y   T
B A M B O O   L I F E B U O Y
U   P   L   A   F   E   P
R E A C T I O N   A R A B I C
N   G   N   D   I   R   A
S I E S T A   S T R I D E N T
```

## No. 8

```
  F I S H A N D C H I P S
O   L   P   T   U   E   O
B R A V A D O   M O N S O O N
I   P   N   N   A   B   R   E
T O P S I D E   S H A L L O W
E   E   E   T   N   A   A
R U R A L   I N T H E S W I M
D       M   H       S
I N T E R F E R E   I N L E T
C   O   E   R   C   I   E
T R U D G E S   E L E C T O R
U   R   R   T   W   B   O   D
M O I D O R E   I N E R T I A
S   U   R   T   R   E   M
S T E P O N T H E G A S
```

**5,** 14 *a.*: Boxer, the noble carthorse in Orwell's *Animal Farm*.

**6,** 21 *a.*: CH(apter) 1/C;   27 *a.*: Lady Sneerwell, *School for Scandal*;
5 *d.*: Also spelt coal-tit.

**8,** 1 *a.*: IF (rev.) + S(H AND C)HIPS;   21 *a.*: Barnaby Rudge;
7 *d.*: O + B(I(n)TERDICT)UM.

## No. 9

```
H A D D O C K ▓ S U B L I M E
O ▓ I ▓ I ▓ U   R N ▓     N
R A S E D ▓ C O M E A B O U T
S ▓ T ▓ F ▓ K ▓ M ▓ C ▓ R ▓ E
E N A M E L ▓ D E F E N D E R
R ▓ F ▓ L ▓ A ▓ R ▓ ▓   E
A W F U L ▓ C A T A M A R A N
C ▓ ▓ O ▓ C ▓ I ▓ E ▓ ▓   U
E L B O W R O O M ▓ N I G H T
  E ▓ ▓ U ▓ E D L ▓   R
D E A D L I N E ▓ R I M I N I
E ▓ G ▓ I ▓ T ▓ R ▓ C ▓ M ▓ M
G O L D E N A G E ▓ A M P L E
A ▓ E ▓ G ▓ N ▓ A ▓ N ▓ S ▓ N
S U S P E C T ▓ P A T I E N T
```

## No. 10

```
W O L F R A M ▓ P A L M I S T
A ▓ O ▓ E ▓ A ▓ A ▓ I ▓     A
P L U N D E R E D ▓ B A T I K
I ▓ T ▓ O ▓ S ▓   R ▓ E ▓ E
T R I A L ▓ H Y D R A N G E A
I ▓ S ▓ E ▓ M ▓ E ▓ E ▓     W
▓ P H A N T A S M A G O R I A ▓
A ▓ C ▓ L ▓ O ▓ Y ▓     Y
T H R E E B L I N D M I C E
O ▓ A ▓ O ▓ S ▓ N ▓ H ▓     P
M O T H E R W I T ▓ A R I E L
I ▓ T ▓ P ▓ R ▓ S ▓ C ▓     U
S Y L P H ▓ B O A T T R A I N
E ▓ E ▓ O ▓ U ▓ T ▓ I ▓     G
R E R E D O S ▓ E N C L O S E
```

## No. 11

```
P R O O F ▓ J U S T I N I A N
A ▓ W ▓ L ▓ O ▓ E ▓ N ▓     U
S U N B A T H E R ▓ D A T E D
S ▓ E ▓ T ▓ N P ▓ E ▓ G
E R R A T A ▓ R E H E A R S E
N ▓ E ▓ H ▓ N ▓ D ▓ L
G R A S S R O O T S ▓ P I T H
E ▓ S ▓ T ▓ N ▓ I ▓ C ▓ N E
R A C K ▓ D O W N M A R K E T
  E ▓ M U ▓ E ▓ R ▓ E
C E N T A U R S ▓ W O N D E R
H ▓ S ▓ S A ▓ P U ▓ R O
A M I S S ▓ B R A S S B A N D
R ▓ O ▓ I ▓ L ▓ I E ▓ W O
M A N S F I E L D ▓ R E L A X
```

## No. 12

```
M A L I C E ▓ A B D I C A T E
E ▓ E H K ▓ Y ▓ N S S
D E T R I M E N T ▓ C L U C K
I ▓ H C E ▓ H U N I
C H E C K U P ▓ E A R L D O M
A ▓ A A O ▓ S E O
L I N E D ▓ N O A H S A R K
S ▓ E E M U I
▓ L I C E N S E E ▓ C H A I N
I L ▓ H T C M C
S U L T A N A ▓ O V E R A L L
L ▓ W N N K S T I
A L I E N ▓ D R E S S D O W N
N L O I N O R E
D E L A Y I N G ▓ B R A Y E D
```

**9,** 1 *d.*: Race of horses in Swift's *Gulliver's Travels*.

**10,** 23 *a.*: In *The Tempest* Prospero frees Ariel from a cloven pine; 8 *d.*: Augustus in Heinrich Hoffmann's *Struwwelpeter*.

**11,** 4 *d.*: Augustus John, John Constable.

**12,** 20 *a.*: Initial letters: 'Can Have Almost Incredible Novelties'; 19 *d.*: Will (verb) = bequeath.

**No. 13**

| D | E | S | O | L | A | T | I | O | N | | | D | | D |
| N | | V | | L | | N | | E | N | T | R | E | E | |
| S | C | R | E | W | I | N | G | | S | | A | | | S |
| O | | R | | E | | R | E | S | T | C | U | R | E | |
| R | | T | | N | A | | | A | | G | | | C | |
| M | E | N | U | | A | L | T | O | G | E | T | H | E | R |
| A | | R | | T | | E | | O | | T | | A | | |
| N | E | M | E | S | I | S | | O | V | E | R | S | E | T |
| I | | O | | O | | G | E | | E | | | E | | E |
| P | A | N | H | A | N | D | L | E | R | | P | R | O | D |
| U | | E | | | I | | | N | | R | | S | | |
| L | A | Y | A | B | O | U | T | | M | | I | | I | |
| A | | B | | L | | | | T | R | E | A | S | U | R | E |
| T | R | O | I | K | A | | E | | N | | A | | I | |
| E | | X | | F | I | R | S | T | C | L | A | S | S | |

**No. 14**

| B | A | L | D | R | I | C | | C | O | T | E | R | I | E |
| U | | A | | A | | A | | O | | H | | U | | X |
| R | O | P | E | D | | P | A | P | E | R | C | L | I | P |
| T | | L | | I | | R | | S | | E | | E | | R |
| H | E | A | V | I | S | I | D | E | | S | E | R | G | E |
| E | | N | | | C | | | H | | | | | S | |
| N | A | D | I | R | | O | U | T | G | O | I | N | G | S |
| E | | | | O | | R | | E | | L | | I | | |
| P | Y | R | O | M | A | N | I | A | | D | O | G | M | A |
| R | | A | | | R | | | H | | | | B | | |
| O | S | C | A | N | | L | A | S | T | R | I | T | E | S |
| S | | A | | T | | A | | H | | O | | M | | T |
| P | A | R | T | Y | L | I | N | E | | D | I | A | N | A |
| E | | E | | P | | R | | E | | I | | R | | I |
| R | E | T | R | E | A | D | | T | I | N | T | E | R | N |

**No. 15**

| S | E | C | R | E | T | S | E | R | V | I | C | E | | |
| T | | H | | G | A | A | | O | | U | | A | | |
| A | N | A | T | O | M | I | S | T | | N | E | P | A | L |
| M | | I | | C | | N | | I | A | | H | | F | |
| P | U | R | S | E | | T | O | N | E | | F | O | U | R |
| I | | N | | L | | G | | F | | R | | | E | |
| N | I | G | H | T | L | Y | | S | T | A | B | B | E | D |
| G | | O | | R | | | | M | | I | | T | | |
| G | R | O | P | I | U | S | | S | P | I | N | A | C | H |
| R | | S | | C | | T | | O | | L | | | E | |
| O | D | E | R | | G | A | L | A | | Y | O | U | N | G |
| U | | S | | S | | T | | N | T | | S | | R | |
| N | O | T | C | H | | U | N | D | E | R | L | I | N | E |
| D | | E | | O | | T | | S | | E | | N | | A |
| | P | I | E | C | E | S | O | F | E | I | G | H | T | |

**No. 16**

| A | L | T | E | R | E | G | O | | S | P | I | N | E | T |
| N | | R | | I | | R | | A | | R | | A | | H |
| T | R | U | S | S | | O | U | T | F | I | T | T | E | R |
| I | | E | | K | | W | | T | | N | | A | | O |
| P | E | N | N | Y | W | I | S | E | | C | O | L | O | N |
| O | | | | O | | N | | N | | I | | E | | |
| P | E | R | I | W | I | G | | D | E | P | U | T | Y | |
| E | | T | | I | | | | L | | A | | G | | |
| | S | H | I | N | E | R | | T | H | E | R | M | A | L |
| C | | | | D | | E | | R | | | | E | | A |
| R | E | M | U | S | | P | L | A | S | T | E | R | E | D |
| I | | U | | C | | A | | V | | R | | L | | N |
| M | E | S | S | A | L | I | N | A | | A | L | A | T | E |
| E | | I | | L | | R | | I | | I | | N | | S |
| A | R | C | H | E | R | | F | L | A | N | D | E | R | S |

**14,** 11 *a*.: Oliver Heaviside, English physicist;    17 *d*.: Mare = dark, flat area on moon.

**15,** 9 *a*.: *The Anatomist*, play by James Bridie;    23 *a*.: Brigham Young; 20 *d*.: Homophones SOW and SEW.

**16,** 15 *d*.: Sellafield, formerly Windscale;    24 *d*.: 'Ride a cock horse...'

## No. 17

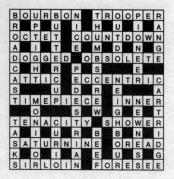

## No. 18

## No. 19

## No. 20

**17,** 21 *d.*: NEW = quarters/head = NESS;  25 *d.*: British Expeditionary Force.

**18,** 26 *a.*: Joshua, the son of Nun;  3 *d.*: Job Trotter (*Pickwick Papers*).

**19,** 5 *a.*: Bab, pen name of W.S. Gilbert.

## No. 21

| S | T | R | I | P | E |   | B | A | L | A | N | C | E | D |
|---|---|---|---|---|---|---|---|---|---|---|---|---|---|---|
| C |   | E |   | A |   | C |   | D |   | U |   | O |   | E |
| R | E | V | I | S | A | L |   | O | A | R | S | M | E | N |
| A |   | E |   | S |   | A |   | R |   | A |   | P |   | S |
| P | A | R | L | I | A | M | E | N | T |   | J | U | T | E |
| B |   | E |   | O |   |   |   | M |   | S |   | T |   |   |
| O | R | D | I | N | A | L |   | E | N | T | R | E | A | T |
| O |   |   | A |   | A |   | N |   | A |   |   | E |   |   |
| K | N | I | T | T | E | R |   | T | A | L | L | I | N | N |
|   | N |   | E |   | C |   |   | A |   | T |   | S |   |   |
| C | U | F | F |   | R | E | T | R | O | G | R | A | D | E |
| O |   | A |   | P |   | N |   | A |   | M |   | L |   | N |
| B | E | N | G | A | L | I |   | C | U | I | S | I | N | E |
| R |   | T |   | I |   | S |   | E |   | T |   | A |   | S |
| A | L | A | C | R | I | T | Y |   | T | E | N | N | I | S |

## No. 22

| L | O | C | U | S |   | F | L | O | O | R | S | H | O | W |
|---|---|---|---|---|---|---|---|---|---|---|---|---|---|---|
| O |   | A |   | T |   | O |   | V |   | E |   | A |   | E |
| A | D | M | I | R | A | B | L | E |   | M | O | R | S | E |
| D |   | E |   | I |   | S |   | R |   | O |   | R |   | N |
| S | T | O | C | K | Y |   | P | R | E | V | I | O | U | S |
| T |   |   | E |   | P |   | I |   | E |   | V |   |   |   |
| O | S | C | A | R | W | I | L | D E |   | L | I | M | B |
| N |   | A |   | S |   | A |   | D |   | S |   | A |   | I |
| E | E | L | S |   | U | N | D | E | R | L | I | N | E | N |
|   |   | E |   | P |   | O |   | N |   | O |   |   | O |
| P | O | N | D | L | I | F | E |   | A | P | E | D | O | M |
| A |   | D |   | I |   | O |   | M |   | S |   | W |   | I |
| S | W | U | N | G |   | R | O | U | G | H | H | E | W | N |
| T |   | L |   | H |   | T |   | S |   | O |   | L |   | A |
| E | N | A | C | T | M | E | N | T |   | P | E | T | A | L |

## No. 23

| H | A | R | R | I | S |   | U | N | I | V | E | R | S | E |
|---|---|---|---|---|---|---|---|---|---|---|---|---|---|---|
|   | C |   | A |   | I |   | N |   | A |   | E |   | X |   |
| S | A | R | D | O | N | I | C |   | P | R | O | M | P | T |
|   | D |   | I |   | G |   | O |   | I |   | O |   | O |   |
| B | E | F | A | L | L | E | N |   | B | A | R | T | E | R |
|   | M |   | T |   | E |   | D |   | N |   | E |   | T |   |
| I |   | O | U | T | R | I | G | H | T |   | L |   | E |   |
| S | C | A | R |   | O |   | T |   | I |   | B | Y | R | D |
| E |   | L |   | I | N | S | I | G | N | I | A |   | E |   |
| N |   | A |   | N |   | O |   | D |   | R |   | E |   |   |
| S | O | C | C | E | R |   | N | O | S | T | R | U | M | S |
| I |   | A |   | R |   | A |   | I |   | E |   | E |   |   |
| B | E | R | A | T | E |   | L | I | G | A | T | U | R | E |
| L |   | T |   | I |   | L |   | H |   | T |   | G |   |   |
| E | L | E | G | A | N | C | Y |   | T | I | E | R | E | D |

## No. 24

| R | E | D | H | A | N | D | E | D |   | M | E | D | O | C |
|---|---|---|---|---|---|---|---|---|---|---|---|---|---|---|
| E |   | U |   | L |   | R |   | U |   | A |   | E |   | H |
| P | A | N | D | O | R | A |   | G | A | L | I | C | I | A |
| R |   | C |   | P |   | U |   | O |   | L |   | A |   | I |
| I | S | E | R | E |   | G | A | U | L | E | I | T | E | R |
| M |   |   | C |   | H |   | T |   | T |   | H |   |   |   |
| A | P | P | O | I | N | T | S |   |   | P | L | U | S |   |
| N |   | E |   | A |   | S |   | C |   | A |   | O |   | U |
| D | A | T | E |   | D | O | O | R | K | N | O | B |   |   |
|   | T |   | M |   | R |   | V |   | M |   |   | E |   |   |
| S | L | I | D | E | R | U | L | E |   | A | S | K | E | D |
| A |   | C |   | D |   | M |   | T |   | T |   | N |   | I |
| T | R | O | L | L | O | P |   | O | P | U | L | E | N | T |
| I |   | A |   | E |   | U |   | U |   | R |   | A |   | O |
| N | A | T | T | Y |   | S | U | S | P | E | N | D | E | R |

**22,** 18 *d.*: Slop, slang for a policeman.

**24,** 6 *a.*: DOME(STI)C;    28 *a.*: Natty Bumppo, the deerslayer in the novels of J. Fenimore Cooper.

## No. 25

```
O X F O R D S T R E E T █
P   A   A   E   E   A   P   A
E S T I M A T E D   G R O U P
N   E   I   H   O   L   L   P
I N S U L T   S U R E F I R E
N   E       B     S     N
G A M B I T   S L I P S H O D
  A   E   L   E   E   E
A R T I S T I C   A N T R I M
T   E   L     P     I
T U R N S O L E   B U L B U L
A   I   E   I   F   S   I   K
C H A I R   P I L C H A R D S
K   L   A   U   A   E   C   O
  D I C T A T O R S H I P
```

## No. 26

```
B L U B B E R   R E V I S E D
O   P   A   O   O   I   N   R
O U S E L   S U P E R N O V A
M   U   A   E   E   G   R   I
E N R I C H   A L G O N K I N
R   G   L   J   A       E
A R E C A   O L D R O W L E Y
N   V   L   D   I       A
G R I S A I L L E   L I L A C
  M   Y   R   E   A   H
D E M E R A R A   A D D I C T
U   E   U   O   S   S   C   S
P E N D R A G O N   I L I U M
I   S   A   E   I   L   S   A
N E E D L E R   P I K E M A N
```

## No. 27

```
S E N S A T I O N   L I G H T
M   U   M   D   O   A   L   R
A C R E A G E   B A R R A G E
L   S   T   A   A   V   D   S
L I E G E   L U L L A B I E S
T   U   I   L   E   A
I N T E R E S T   S T A R
M   R   S   T   S   P   O   E
E L A T   T E A R D R O P
  N   M   B   W   O     R
D I S C O U R S E   S H A M E
O   P   T   I   R   P   D   S
S T O W I N G   A N E M O N E
E   R   O   H   G   C   R   N
S A T I N   T R E A T M E N T
```

## No. 28

```
S T A R C H   A M I C A B L E
A   R   H   C   A   O   A   P
P E T T I C O A T   L I N G O
I   I   N   M   R   E   D   N
E X C L A I M   O D Y S S E Y
N   L   W   I   N   A   M
C H E L A   S H O W D O W N
E       R   S   F   E     B
  F E V E R I S H   B I J O U
R   M   O   O   U   O   R
E V A S I O N   N O T H I N G
L   N   L   A   O   A   N   U
I R A Q I   I G U A N O D O N
E   T   A   R   R   T   E   D
F L E T C H E R █ B E T R A Y
```

**25,** 1 *a*.: Exeter and Lincoln – Oxford colleges;     19 *a*.: AN(OTHER) + TRIM;     2 *d*.: F + odd letters removed from 'fast news'.

**26,** 15 *a*.: Charles II's nickname, from his favourite stallion;
27 *a*.: Marlowe's *Dr Faustus*;     8 *d*.: Arsenal, the Gunners = RA;     22 *d*.: Dupin, E.A. Poe's French detective.

**27,** 6 *d*.: LAR/V/AE (pen name of G.W. Russell, Irish poet) – larvae = spectre, ghost.

**28,** 18 *a*.: F.E. Smith, Lord Birkenhead.

**No. 29**

```
R O O F T R E E   P O R T L Y
O   P   R   X   R   O   U
S T E R E O T Y P E   S A C K
E   N   A   I   C   E   E
B R E A D A N D B U T T E R
U   N   E   C   R   T   N
D I D E R O T   E S C A P E E
  E   D   O   E
A D D E N D A   B R I S T L E
  E   N   J   O   N   T   N
  W I N D O W D R E S S I N G
  D   O   B   E   T   C   L
C R A B   M A N D R A G O R A
  O   L   A   O   L   A   N
S P L E E N   E M U L A T E D
```

**No. 30**

```
P R E S E N T A T I O N
U   X   P   E   R   X   L   S
M A C H I N A T E   E D I C T
P   E   C   L   A   Y   N   A
K I L T E R   A S P E R I T Y
I   N   N   U   M   E
N U D I T Y   D R U M H E A D
  I   R   D   E   O   N
R U N N E R U P   P O O T E R
E   O   C   N   E
P A S T I C H E   P L A C I D
A   A   S   E   R   I   H   C
S P U R S   S H A N G R I L A
T   R   U   S   G   H   D   P
  B E N E F A C T R E S S
```

**No. 31**

```
M I S A D V E N T U R E
I   T   E   D   I   A   M   L
C O R N F I E L D   V O I C E
R   A   O   N   E   E   S   S
O R W E L L   E M U L A T E S
B   I   A   R   E
E N D E A R   P R E S S U R E
  R   N   B   K   U   S
S P E C T R U M   S N A T C H
O   D   D   D   A
R E G I C I D E   P E S T E R
E   E   L   L   F   R   R   N
L A R G O   E R A D I C A T E
Y   S   T   I   I   N   D   S
  T H E A T R E G O E R S
```

**No. 32**

```
S C O T C H M I S T   M A I L
O   S   O   I   O   M   A
H A L F M I L E R S   S E W N
O   O   M   A   T   P   L   D
  M O O N L I G H T I N G
C   R   N   L   I   O   R
O V E R W R O T E   L O R C A
N   G   E   F   G   H   A   V
S I E N A   F R E M A N T L E
E   N   L   C   R   E   S
Q U E S T I O N T I M E
U   R   H   L   H   O   P   T
E D A M   M O T I O N L E S S
N   T   U   R   I   K   A
T H E M   C R I D E C O E U R
```

**30,** 18 *a.*: Blue runner, American Atlantic fish.

**32,** 18 *a.*: Burnt Sienna.

## No. 33

| J | A | C | K | A | N | A | P | E | S | | S | T | O | P |
| A | | O | | F | | C | | X | | D | | W | | R |
| B | E | N | E | F | I | T | | P | R | I | V | A | T | E |
| O | | S | | E | | R | | U | | V | | N | | S |
| T | R | U | N | C | H | E | O | N | | E | A | G | L | E |
| | | L | | T | | S | | G | | R | | | | N |
| I | R | A | Q | I | | S | W | E | E | T | M | E | A | T |
| N | | T | | O | | | | I | | | N | | | E |
| S | T | E | R | N | P | O | S | T | | S | I | T | E | D |
| T | | | | A | | R | | R | | | S | | | R |
| A | D | M | I | T | | B | O | O | M | E | R | A | N | G |
| N | | A | | E | | I | | U | | | M | | N | R |
| T | R | I | O | L | E | T | | B | R | E | S | C | I | A |
| E | | Z | | Y | | | E | L | | N | | E | | S |
| R | H | E | A | | A | D | V | E | R | T | I | S | E | S |

## No. 34

| A | B | S | E | N | T | M | I | N | D | E | D | | | |
| G | | E | | U | | A | | A | | A | | C | | A |
| O | L | D | S | T | A | G | E | R | | S | L | O | O | P |
| N | | G | | R | | I | | R | | E | | M | | P |
| I | R | E | N | I | C | | H | A | N | D | M | A | D | E |
| S | | | | S | | M | | T | | | N | | A | |
| T | U | R | N | E | R | | P | O | E | T | I | C | A | L |
| | E | | N | | M | | R | | | I | | H | | |
| S | E | D | A | T | I | O | N | | A | T | T | E | N | D |
| U | | R | | | U | | | H | | | R | | | |
| F | R | A | G | M | E | N | T | | B | E | R | T | H | A |
| F | | F | | I | | T | | O | | B | | W | | G |
| E | X | T | O | L | | A | C | T | U | A | T | I | O | N |
| R | | | S | | E | | I | | | R | | N | | E |
| | | | T | R | A | N | S | C | E | N | D | E | N | T |

## No. 35

| L | A | W | N | M | O | W | E | R | | C | U | B | E | S |
| A | | A | | O | | E | | O | | O | | O | | T |
| U | P | S | I | L | O | N | | W | A | R | B | L | E | R |
| R | | P | | L | | S | | | | A | | O | | E |
| A | D | I | E | U | | L | I | M | E | L | I | G | H | T |
| | | S | | S | | E | | E | | | | N | | C |
| A | S | H | | C | R | Y | P | T | O | G | R | A | P | H |
| L | | | A | | D | | R | | I | | | | E | |
| L | A | M | E | N | T | A | T | I | O | N | | F | U | R |
| E | | I | | L | | | C | | P | | L | | | |
| V | E | N | E | Z | U | E | L | A | | A | L | O | U | D |
| I | | A | | E | | | T | | L | | R | | A | |
| A | C | R | O | B | A | T | | I | T | A | L | I | A | N |
| T | | E | | R | | I | | O | | C | | S | | D |
| E | X | T | R | A | | P | U | N | G | E | N | T | L | Y |

## No. 36

| S | T | U | R | G | E | O | N | | B | O | T | T | O | M |
| A | | P | | U | | N | | S | | R | | R | | I |
| N | A | S | A | L | | E | M | A | N | A | T | I | O | N |
| D | | E | | C | | R | | N | | N | | P | | U |
| W | A | T | C | H | W | O | R | D | | G | H | E | N | T |
| I | | | | T | | | U | | R | | U | | | E |
| C | U | I | R | A | S | S | | A | T | T | E | S | T | |
| H | | N | | R | | | A | | Q | | | | R | |
| | E | G | G | C | U | P | | C | O | N | F | U | S | E |
| F | | | | H | | A | | R | | | E | | V | |
| A | O | R | T | A | | R | E | I | N | S | T | A | T | E |
| T | | O | | N | | I | | M | | H | | M | | R |
| H | O | U | R | G | L | A | S | S | | A | L | I | V | E |
| O | | N | | E | | H | | O | R | | S | | N | |
| M | I | D | D | L | E | | S | N | A | P | S | H | O | T |

**33,** 13 *a.*: Code name for lunar module in 1969 moon landing;
1 *d.*: JAB/(B)OT(H).

**35,** 26 *a.*: Rossini's *The Italian Girl in Algiers.*

**36,** 22 *d.*: Mark Twain = leadsman's call for two fathoms.

**No. 37**

```
P A W P A W   S O M E B O D Y
  M   E A T   O   E     O
F O U R I N H A N D   I A G O
  U   C   D   R   E   N   C
A R C H N E S S   R E G I O N
    A   R     A   A   L
O P E N   N U T S H E L L
  R   C   P   D   E   I   A
S I B E L I U S   S O R E
  V     N   T   S   T
R A I S I N   R A T I O N A L
  T   I   A   I   E   R   Z
D E E M   C O P E R N I C U S
  E   O   L   E   N   E   R
P R I N C E S S   A N S W E R
```

**No. 38**

```
J E H A D   H O R S E W H I P
A   O R O   I   R   A   A
C O M E A L O N G   R E V E L
K   E   F   D   H A   E   M
K A R A T E   S T I N G R A Y
E       I   I   A   D S
T O U R N A M E N T   H A W K
C   P   G   P G   M   C   I
H O S E   M E A L T I C K E T
A     E   D   E   D       C
P E D A N T I C   S N A T C H
O   A   I   M   S   I   O E
L Y I N G   E N L I G H T E N
Y   S   M   N   U   H E   E
P A Y M A S T E R   T I M E R
```

**No. 39**

```
P E E V E   E X T I R P A T E
O   L   S C A   E   L   M
L I G H T S H I P   C L O S E
E   A   O   O D   E   N   N
M A R I N A   B A N D A G E D
I     I   F   N   E S
C O C K A T R I C E   K I N D
A   O   N   A E   H   D   I
L O L L   S T U R D I N E S S
L     S   R   S G   C
P L A N T A I N   S H I N T O
A   R   R   C S   R   A   V
C A I R O   I M P R O V I S E
T   N   N   D I   A   A   R
S A G E G R E E N   D A D D Y
```

**No. 40**

```
M I S A D V E N T U R E
E   E   O A   A   U O   R
T E C H N I C A L   F O R G O
H   C   A   H L   F   G   O
O P O R T O   H Y D E P A R K
D       E   M       N   I
S A D D L E   G E R M A I N E
E   L   B   N   O S
B A L M O R A L   R U S T L E
O   I   S   S       N
D O V E T A I L   W E I G H T
I   E   Y   L A   T   U   E
C A R O L   D E S E R T I O N
E   Y   E   O T   A   S   T
  F R O N T I S P I E C E
```

**38,** 4 *a*.: With it = trendy, hip;  11 *a*.: Kate Greenaway, English illustrator;  18 *d*.: M(1 DN)IGHT.

**40,** 12 *a*.: Mungo Park;  22 *d*.: Wat and John.

**No. 41**

**No. 42**

**No. 43**

**No. 44**

**41,** 20 *a.*: Song, 'Won't you come home, Bill Bailey?'

**43,** 28 *a.*: Sir Kay, King Arthur's steward;  2 *d.*: April, May, June;
6 *d.*: Lupin Pooter, *Diary of a Nobody*.

**44,** 15 *a.*: Hero, or Heron, Greek mathematician of the first century
AD;  21 *a.*: 'Pippa Passes', Robert Browning.

## No. 45

```
W R A T H   R I C E P A P E R
A   D   I   O   H   A   I   A
S H O R T W A V E   T U N I C
H   P   I   D   V   H   C   E
E N T I T Y   B R E A T H E R
D       O   C   O   N   B
O U T O F S O R T S   H E A T
U   H   F   M   A   D   C   H
T E R N   P E R I W I N K L E
E   C   H   N   S
D E S P O T I C   S P I D E R
R   H   N   T   P   A   R   I
A L O O F   H E A R T L E S S
W   L   A   E   S   C   A   E
S I D E B U R N S   H A D E S
```

## No. 46

```
H E R I T A G E   D I S A R M
O   E   U   E     N   L     A
B U L L R I N G   F L A C O N
S   I   N   E   E   A   A   D
O A S I S   R O S E W A T E R
N   H   T   A   C     R   I
    B I L L I A R D B A L L
C   P   L   I   P   I   Z   L
U P O N E S S L E E V E
T   S   S   C   E   S   M
S P I R I T U A L   R O U S E
H   T   L   E   A   S   P   T
O R I G I N   F U G I T I V E
R   V   A     S   O   N   O
T R E N D Y   R E I N D E E R
```

## No. 47

```
P S A L M I S T   C A P E R S
A   N   I   W   H   A   E
P O T E N T I L L A   R O P E
Y   I   O   N   R   A   U
R E C O R D I N G A N G E L
U   L   C   S   B   O   S
S P I N A C H   L A U N D E R
N   A   N   E
B R E W E R S   A C H A T E S
A   E   P   W   O   E   U
F A L S E P R E T E N C E S
F   L   N   S   D   T   P
L I D O   T H E O D O L I T E
S   F   R   M   W   V   C
S H I F T Y   R E I N V E S T
```

## No. 48

```
S C O T F R E E   P U L P I T
H   I   E   T   A   R   R
H A G G L E   E X C U S E M E
P   H   F   R   K   S   A
S L A T T E R N   I M P E L S
E   S   R   A   T   N   U
S T E P S   A L L I G A T O R
U   O   S   T   N   U   E
S T A T U T O R Y   A N G E R
P   N   A   I   T   M
E L I X I R   A B R A S I O N
N   S   F   N   I   A   T
D W E L L I N G   P A L L I D
E   E   S   L   L   O
R A D I S H   E V E R Y O N E
```

**45,** 14 *a.*: Sorts = founts, characters;  29 *a.*: Alternate letters of 'The address'.

**46,** 4 *d.*: General issue = a simple denial of the whole charge (law).

**47,** 14 *d.*: Chief Detective Inspector French, F. Wills Crofts.

## No. 49

```
F I D D L E S T I C K S ■ ■
E   R   O   O   N   E   E   M
D R A G H O U N D ■ B A S S O
E   F   E   L   I   A   P   N
R A T I N G ■ S C A B B A R D
A   G   ■ A     L     A
L A B A R A ■ A T R O C I T Y
A   I   R   E   V   E
D E C A N T E R ■ P E E R E D
R   T   C     R     E
O V E R T A K E ■ S T R O L L
V   R   I   L   I   U   L   I
E L I O T ■ E N D O R S I N G
R   A   L   S   L   N   V   H
■ ■ R E A S S E S S M E N T
```

## No. 50

```
M A P L E S ■ S T A N D A R D
A   A   R   S   O   E   D   R
R A N S A C K ■ R E S T O R E
G   A   D   Y   M   T   R   A
A R C H I M E D E S ■ F I R M
R   H   C     N   M   N
I R E L A N D ■ T R I G G E R
N   T   I   O   N     E
E N D L E S S ■ R O U N D U P
O   D   C     T   E   E
P A C E ■ J O U R N E Y M A N
A   K   M   U   O   H   E   T
S T A T I O N ■ S W A N S E A
T   G   E   T   E   N   N   N
E V E N N E S S ■ A D V E N T
```

## No. 51

```
I N A U D I B L E ■ T H I E F
N   R   I   R   N   H   N   O
C O M E S T O ■ D R E S S E R
A   Y   T   T   I   G   R
S H A R E ■ H Y D R A N G E A
■ N   M   E   E     H   T
R O T ■ P U R P L E P A T C H
E   E   H   E   A   E
P A T E R N O S T E R ■ M A R
E   O   O   E   T   U
R E M A I N D E R ■ H E T U P
T   B   B   I   E   A   O
O P O S S U M ■ O M N I B U S
R   L   E   U   U   O   L   I
Y E A R N ■ D I S I N F E C T
```

## No. 52

```
L I T O T E S ■ P O T H E R B
O   E   U   A   L   A   L   U
W A R B L E F L Y ■ S W E L L
E   R   I   E   S   G   L
S T A M P ■ T E C T O N I C S
T   C   T   Y   H     S   E
■ P E T R O C H E M I S T R Y
T   E   A   E   N     E
W O R C E S T E R S A U C E ■
A   U   C   L   M   H   H
D E B A U C H E E ■ O Z O N E
D   D   P     A   R   C   A
L O O P S ■ M A D H A T T E R
E   W   E   A   E   T   A   T
R I N G T A W ■ R O A D W A Y
```

**49**, 20 *d.*: Song, 'Camptown Races', S.C. Foster.

**51**, 17 *a.*: Paternoster lift;  6 *d.*: 8th letter in Greek alphabet;
19 *d.*: Mu, first letter of Marathon.

**52**, 5 *a.*: Pre-Raphaelite Brotherhood;  17 *a.*: Earl of Worcester, *Henry IV, Part II*;  8 *d.*: Bill Sikes's dog in *Oliver Twist*.

## No. 53

```
P U T T O S H A M E ■ S O A P
O   O   N   U   A   N R   E
T R A D E I N ■ D R E D G E R
T   S   O   D   N   A A   S
O U T O F T R U E ■ R I N S E
R   T   E   S   T   V
C O A C H ■ D I S C H A R G E
U   C   E       E   E R
T A K E S T O C K ■ K N I F E
A   E   V   N   N   T
N A M E D ■ E M O L U M E N T
D   I   A   R   W C   R   I
R E L A Y E D ■ A W K W A R D
U   E   S   I   L L   T   E
N O S E ■ A D U L T E R E S S
```

## No. 54

```
S A M P A N ■ A B S E N T E E
E   A   R   C O   L   A   L
T A R R A G O N A ■ L I B R A
A   B   U   U   R   I   L I
S I L I C O N ■ D I S C E R N
I   E   A   T   I   A   E
D O S E R ■ R U N A B O U T
E   I   Y   G A   C
■ V E R A N D A S ■ N E A T H
S   M   A   C N   M   A
C L U B M A N ■ H E I R E S S
A   L   I   C O   S   N S
L E A R N ■ I N O U T L I N E
E   T   U   N   L E   T   U
D R E S S A G E ■ P R A Y E R
```

## No. 55

```
B R O A D S ■ S H O W D O W N
E   I   H   P   I   U   E
O V E R D O N E ■ I N S T E P
I   C   R   C   T   R   O
A E G R O T A T ■ S E X I S T
W   A   F   A   R   D   I
E   F L A T T E R Y   E S
B R A T ■ L O U ■ P R A M
A   R   F L O R E N C E   P
R   T   I   S A   R   P
B A I L E Y ■ P A R T I C L E
I   F   L   O   O   S   A
C L A U D E ■ R O U G H S U P
A   C   E   T   N   E S
N O T A R I E S ■ D O R S E T
```

## No. 56

```
R E B U T ■ C O P Y R I G H T
E   A   O   A   A I   A   I
F O R G O T T E N ■ V A L E T
R   E   T   W   A E   L   A
E A R T H ■ A S C E R T A I N
S   S   L   H   N
H A D D O C K ■ E S T A T E S
E   E   M   E   R   I
R E T R E A T ■ D E L A Y E D
E   R   E E   E
T I R E D N E S S ■ G R A I L
A   M   E   A S   R   H I
B A I R N ■ C A E S A R E A N
O   N   Y   L   R   P A   E
O V E R S P E N T ■ H A D E S
```

**53,** 7 *d.*: (f)OR + NAG rev.

**54,** 3 *d.*: Monkey (£500) puzzle (enigma) tree;   5 *d.*: *The Pirates of Penzance*, operetta by W.S. Gilbert and Arthur Sullivan.

**55,** 19 *a.*: Michelangelo's sculpture of David.

**57**, 3 *d*.: Beer brewed in October;     18 *d*. Michael Darling, *Peter Pan*.

**59**, 6 *a*.: Captain Ahab in *Moby Dick* and King of Israel;
7, *d*.: Og, King of Bashan.